Tennessee Log Buildings

Tennessee Log Buildings

A Folk Tradition
John B. Rehder

The University of Tennessee Press • Knoxville

Copyright © 2012 by The University of Tennessee Press / Knoxville.
All Rights Reserved. Manufactured in the United States of America.
First Edition.

Illustrations not otherwise credited are courtesy of the author.

The paper in this book meets the requirements of American
National Standards Institute / National Information Standards
Organization specification Z39.48–1992 (Permanence of Paper). It
contains 30 percent post-consumer waste and is certified by the
Forest Stewardship Council.

Library of Congress Cataloging-in-Publication Data

Rehder, John B.
Tennessee log buildings: a folk tradition / John B. Rehder. — 1st ed.
    p. cm.
Includes bibliographical references and index.
ISBN-13: 978-1-57233-874-6 (pbk.: alk. paper)
ISBN-10: 1-57233-874-1 (pbk.: alk. paper)
 1. Log buildings—Tennessee—History.
 2. Log buildings—Tennessee—Design and construction.
 3. Vernacular architecture—Tennessee—History.
 4. Farm buildings—Tennessee—History.
 5. Historic buildings—Tennessee.
 6. Tennessee—Social life and customs.
 7. Tennessee—History, Local.
 I. Title.

NA730.T4R34 2012
721'.044809768—dc23
2012017303

Contents

Preface		xi
Chapter 1	Discovering Folk Architecture	1
Chapter 2	Two Tennessee Hearths: A Settlement History	25
Chapter 3	Log Houses	39
Chapter 4	Log Barns and Outbuildings	83
Chapter 5	Exceptional Log Places	111
Appendix	Distribution Maps	135
References		145
Index		155

Illustrations

FIGURES

Tennessee and Its 95 Counties	xiv
Single-Pen Log House in Grainger County	2
Union County Family in 1933	3
Stanley Valley	7
Checking the Meek Williams Site	8
Dogtrot House in Warren County	10
Single Pen in Jefferson County	13
Drilling Core Samples for Dendrochronology	15
Hamblen County Log House Dated to 1812	16
Swaggerty Blockhouse	17
"Wigwam" Log Building at Camp Nakanawa	21
Mud-and-Stick Chimney	23
The Upland South and Lowland South Regions	26
Physiographic Regions of Tennessee	28
Fort Marr	30
Heinrich Ernst House	34
Routes of the Robertson and Donelson Settlement Parties	36
Saddle Notch	44
Saddle-V Notch	45
V Notch	47
Half-Dovetail Notch	48
Full-Dovetail Notch	50
Diamond Notch	51

Different Notch Types in Same Building	52
House Type Evolution	57
Single-Pen House	59
Restored Single Pen in Hawkins County	61
Single-Pen with Half-Dovetail Notches, Putnam County	61
Cumberland House in Middle Tennessee	63
Noah "Bud" Ogle Place, Great Smoky Mountains National Park	65
View of Deteriorating Ogle Place, 1958	66
Dogtrot House, Lewis County	67
Dogtrot House with Enclosed Breezeway	68
John White Dogtrot House	70
I-House, Blount County	73
I-House Converted into Barn, Marshall County	74
Declining Home Place, Fentress County, 1982	75
I-House on Banks of Tennessee River, Loudon	76
Stone I-House, Sumner County	77
Four-Pen House with Log Construction, Maury County	79
Log Bungalow House, Hawkins County	80
Box House, Hawkins County	81
Evolution of Barns	85
Typical Single-Crib, Hardeman County	86
Single-Crib with Gear Shed, Grainger County	87
Saddle-Roof Double-Crib Barn, Clay County	88
Double-Crib Barn with Roof Paralleling Crib's Long Axis	88
Four-Crib Barn at Noah "Bud" Ogle Place	90
Transverse-Crib Barn, Putnam County	91
Cantilever Barn, Sevier County	92
Cantilever Barn, Great Smoky Mountains National Park	93
Sevier County Cantilever Barn	94
Smokehouse, Johnson County	98
Cantilever Smokehouse, Eastern Sevier County	100
Two-Level Smokehouse, Western Sevier County	101
Springhouse, Hawkins County	102
Cellar Outbuilding, Johnson County	103
Granary, Grainger County	105
Blacksmith Shop Built in 1793, Union County	105
Log Church, Morgan County	107
Old Union United Methodist Church, Hawkins County	107
Okolona Church, Overton County	107
Old Union Meeting House, Overton County	109

Stone Mountain School, Hawkins County	110
Walker Springs Place, West Knox County	112
Walker Springs Place after Relocation to South Knox County	113
Marble Springs Plantation, South Knox County	114
Hamilton-Tolliver Place, Union County	117
Central Chimney in Hamilton-Tolliver Place	118
Wynnewood, North Elevation and West Gable End	119
Wynnewood after Tornado	119
View of Wynnewood Showing Dogtrot and Saddlebag Characteristics	120
South Elevation of Wynnewood's Main House	122
V-Notched Oak and Black Walnut Logs, Wynnewood	123
Meek Williams Saddlebag House	125
Meek Williams Barn	126
Center Crib, Meek Williams Barn	128
Museum of Appalachia, Anderson County	132
Great Smoky Mountains Heritage Center, Blount County	133
Restored Log Place, Knox County	133

DISTRIBUTION MAPS

Distribution maps are located in the appendix, beginning on page 135.

Map 1. All Log Houses	Map 18. I-Houses
Map 2. Saddle Notches	Map 19. Four-Pen Houses
Map 3. Saddle-V Notches	Map 20. Bungalow Houses
Map 4. Notches	Map 21. Box Houses
Map 5. Half-Dovetail Notches	Map 22. All Barns and Outbuildings
Map 6. Full-Dovetail Notches	Map 23. Single-Crib Barns
Map 7. Diamond Notches	Map 24. Single-Crib and Gear Sheds
Map 8. Square Notches	Map 25. Double-Crib Barns
Map 9. Double Notches	Map 26. Four-Crib Barns
Map 10. Yellow Poplar Timbers	Map 27. Transverse-Crib Barns
Map 11. Oak Timbers	Map 28. Cantilever Barns
Map 12. Pine Timbers	Map 29. Smokehouses
Map 13. Cedar Timbers	Map 30. Springhouses
Map 14. Single-Pen Houses	Map 31. Granary Buildings
Map 15. Cumberland Houses	Map 32. Blacksmith Shops
Map 16. Saddlebag Houses	Map 33. Church Buildings
Map 17. Dogtrot Houses	Map 34. School Buildings

Preface

This is a project I have wanted to do for quite some time. In 1967, when I was 25 years old, I was hired as an assistant professor by the Department of Geography at the University of Tennessee. Just seven years out of high school, I arrived as a professional cultural geographer fresh from graduate school and eager to explore the landscapes and meet the people of Tennessee. Always curious, I spent weekends dragging my wife and two small children around in a green Chevy Malibu and later in a VW camper bus over bumpy gravel back roads searching for old buildings, especially old log ones, to photograph. As it turns out, my daughter Karen (now an adult) remembers houses now gone that I have long forgotten.

For over four decades, I have explored Tennessee and much of Southern Appalachia, and I am now offering you an opportunity to discover Tennessee's architectural heritage in ways you might never have imagined. The book focuses on historic log architecture in Tennessee. It is based on Tennessee Historical Commission historic buildings survey data for 4,208 log structures in 42 Tennessee counties as well as on my 40 years of field experience exploring Tennessee's rural landscapes.

This book's focus on Tennessee's log buildings expands on chapter 4 of my book *Appalachian Folkways*, which covered 17 Tennessee counties. Covering 42 counties, this new book features data expressed on 34 distribution maps, which are found in the appendix. Chapter 3 refers to 8 maps of corner-notch types, 4 maps of timber types, and 9 maps illustrating county distributions for house types. In chapter 4, there are references to 13 maps that show distributions of barns and outbuildings. The photographs throughout the book constitute a good sample of representative log buildings in Tennessee. As you thumb through the pages, I hope you can appreciate the nature of historic, folk log buildings, will reflect on those you possibly know or grew up around, and will see the unique world that ancestral folks created in Tennessee.

There are so many people to thank. My interests in folk culture and rural settlement stem from mentors and colleagues: long-time friend and mentor Fritz Gritzner, the late Fred B. Kniffen, who was my graduate advisor at Louisiana State University, and the late Terry G. Jordan-Bychkov, a good friend and exceptional colleague. I especially thank Steve Rogers and his staff at the Tennessee Historical Commission in Nashville for access to literally thousands of pieces of data. Many thanks for the many maps go to Tracy Pollock for her fine cartography and to Will Fontanez, director of the University of Tennessee Cartographic Services Laboratory. The Department of Geography and the College of Arts and Sciences at the University of Tennessee contributed valuable field time and small grants for me to build the project. Long hours, long distances, and crackers and sodas for field food were part of the research experience, so any support was most welcome.

A book project has people behind the scenes whose work I greatly appreciate: copyeditors, technical editors, marketing people, and printing folks, among others. The people at the University of Tennessee Press are all special to me. Scot Danforth, UT Press director, editor, and friend, gets particular thanks for his fine work. I also thank Cheryl Carson and Tom Post in marketing, Kerry Webb and Thomas Wells in acquisitions, Stan Ivester and Gene Adair in copyediting, Lisa Davis in the business office, and other folks who have been friends and colleagues for years and who are really wonderful to work with.

My family always gets special recognition. My wife Judy, daughter Karen, son Ken, and daughter-in-law Angie are very special people in my life. Most precious at this time are grandchildren Allen and Emma Caroline, who sometimes assist me in the field. On a trip to the Museum of Appalachia near Norris, Tennessee, the kids helped me take photographs and identify objects around the grounds. Since then, whenever we pass a special rail fence, they yell, "Opa, look, a snake . . . fence!"

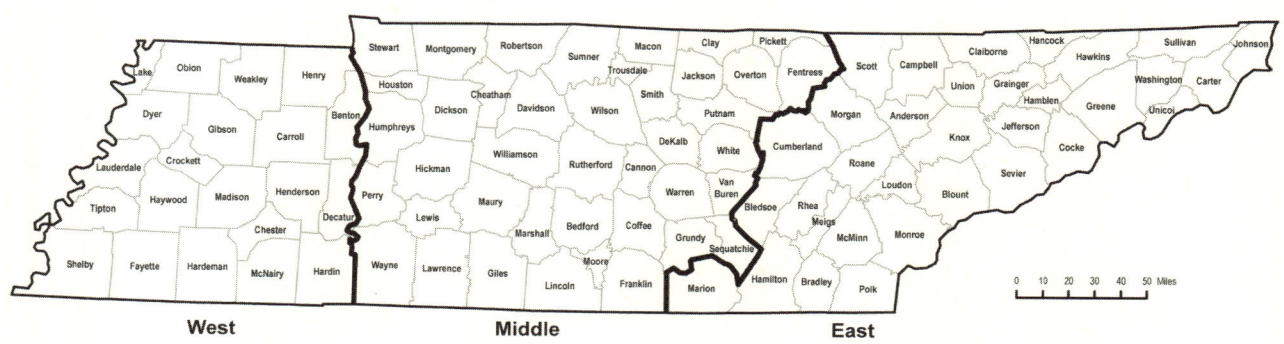

Tennessee, with its 95 counties and three grand divisions indicated.

Chapter 1

Discovering Folk Architecture

Architecture: the very word speaks of more than just houses and other buildings. As a creative art form devoted to the control of space and volume in the built environment, formal architecture focuses on planned structures created from designs by professionally trained architects. Frequently, the markets for architecture of this sort are the people and institutions associated with "high culture"—that is, those who can best afford it. The pursuit of formal, professional architecture can lead to wealth and fame, and, in some people's eyes, signify a certain arrogance among its practitioners and their clients.

In this book, however, I want to explore a different form of architecture, one not found on drafting tables or in plan books, an architecture that includes dirt-floored cabins in places like Southern Appalachia, which are often perceived as backwaters. I refer now to folk architecture, the kind that poor and not-so-poor people have built for centuries through traditional means, planned from daddy's or papaw's or great-granddaddy's mental images and then constructed with hand tools—axes, adzes, froes, drawknives, and the like.

Folk architecture, also called vernacular architecture, comes from traditional, homegrown sources. *Vernacular* in the anthropological sense normally means a native local language or colloquial speech, but it can mean traditional material culture as well. Within the past 40 years, the term *vernacular* when coupled with *architecture* has come to refer to historic buildings hand-built by folks in a folk culture. In recent years, however, vernacular architecture as investigated by the international organization known as the Vernacular Architecture Forum (VAF) has come to include not only folk-culture buildings but also

Our image of a typical log cabin might be like this one, a single-pen log house in Grainger County, photographed in 1978.

journeyman's houses and industrial structures and factories that may have had professional plans. Among the fine folks in the VAF (of which I am a member), there is just as much interest in the historic architecture of an old railroad depot or a textile mill as there is in an authentic folk-built log cabin.

The log buildings featured in this book were constructed in the eighteenth, nineteenth, and twentieth centuries. I examine log structures that were built between 1784 and 1920, some in the 1930s and 1940s, and only a very few built as late as about 1960. Many are in deplorable condition. Some were in ruins when we began our professional surveys of historic structures three decades ago; many structures no longer exist. I know of buildings that neither you nor I would have chosen for shelter even if we had lived in the time and place of their construction. Crude, rough-hewn, drafty—these words describe most log buildings. Lofty, massive, solid, sturdy, and sometimes warm and possibly comfortable just might describe a select few.

An East Tennessee family and their old log house, October 31, 1933. By 1936, the Tennessee Valley Authority had flooded this site in Union County near Loyston during the creation of the Norris Reservoir, the agency's first hydroelectric dam project. (TVA photo courtesy of the Roy Acuff Museum, Maynardville, TN.)

Perhaps your image of log architecture comes from a "Lincoln Logs" toy set you remember from childhood. The log structures in this book rarely have that "Lincoln Log" look. The toy logs are modeled after the double-notch type found in Old World structures in Alpine Europe and Scandinavia. In Tennessee, I know of a few double-notched examples, including summer camp–style cabins built in the 1930s for state parks, as well as some urban houses, but these can hardly be described as "folk."

We have much to explore regarding the types of log buildings and the methods used for locking horizontal logs with corner notches. But before we get into technical specifics (I save that for chapter 3), I should explain folk culture.

FOLK TRADITIONS

Folk things are traditional. They are homemade, built from oral instructions, and handed down through the generations. In folk culture, if your daddy followed grandpa's advice, you too would likely follow and practice the sage oral messages passed on to you. Folk log buildings arrive without blueprints. Coming from traditional memory, folk structures are planned in a way very different from that of formal architecture. Forms and floor plans are passed down from generation

Discovering Folk Architecture

to generation. Such architectural processes and patterns are analogous to a folk song learned by ear and played on a homemade banjo, as opposed to a professionally written composition performed by a formally trained musician on a Steinway piano. Tradition rules in folk culture; creative logic comes in a distant second (Rehder 2004, 15–17).

Authentic folk-house types are much more than dirt-floored, one-room cabins, and they reflect diagnostic traits through their form, function, and construction. And folk houses do not have to be built of logs to be folk: they can be built of stone, brick, or sawn, framed lumber. In this book, however, I am emphasizing log construction because it is integral to understanding folk architecture in Appalachia in general and Tennessee in particular. Log construction from the eighteenth, nineteenth, and part of the twentieth centuries became a crucial surrogate for folk culture and folk architecture in Southern Appalachia. Virtually anything built of logs before 1960 is potentially a folk building. We will examine the old folkways of log construction that were common in Tennessee in the years from about 1769 to 1880, a major period of home-built, folk architecture dominated by the use of logs. When saw-milled lumber became widely available after the 1880s, the use of logs for home construction declined. A short-term resurgence of log houses occurred in the 1930s when needy rural folk built "Depression houses" with small-diameter pine logs using saddle and saddle-V notches. While these temporary dwellings in the Great Depression years were indeed folk houses, the quality of workmanship and available materials was frequently inferior to that of nineteenth-century log structures. The post–World War II years between 1945 and 1960 saw a number of barns built of round logs. Known as "pole barns," they would be the last of folk log construction in any form in the region. After 1970, commercial companies began erecting brand new log buildings using timber species from western states. Most companies now cut half-dovetail notches on hewn logs in their structures, and this notch type represents the closest connection between historic, traditional log homes and contemporary ones.

Since we are focusing on historic folk architecture, I make a point to avoid the commercial log architecture that came after the 1970s. Commercially built log houses are neither folk nor are they built with native timber. Modern log-house builders in the Southeast are numerous; they include such firms as the Barna Company near Oneida in Scott County, Tennessee, and the Honest Abe log house factory at Moss in Clay County, Tennessee. In the vicinity of Knoxville, there are 15 companies that build log homes. Log-home companies offer colorful brochures and attractive designs, including modern cabins and multiroom mansions. These manufactured log homes are weather-tight with effective gaskets in the chinking and logs from species such as lodge pole pine, western spruce, and Douglas fir. The structures often fulfill the dreams of people who want to own a log home. I am content that such interest in modern log architecture exists. But examining this kind of log architecture is not my purpose here.

FIELDWORK DISCOVERY

Traditional folk architecture, especially in log construction, frequently illustrates the personality of a place and the personality of its folk builders. In this book, we shall explore Tennessee's relic cultural landscapes in the context of first effective settlement and the imprint of log construction in notch types, house types, barn types, and small outbuildings. This excursion cannot be comprehensive because the survey of historic buildings in Tennessee is still a work in progress. As of 2006, 66 of Tennessee's 95 counties had been surveyed, were being surveyed, or were planned for historic-building surveys by teams working for the Tennessee Historical Commission (THC). My task here is to analyze and interpret the data collected in 42 counties so as to illustrate the types of log architecture in Tennessee that represent much of the state's settlement history. In addition to analyzing data on 4,208 log buildings, this book also includes four up-close-and-personal case studies. While there are excellent books written on historic folk architecture in North Carolina, Kentucky, and Alabama, I know of no state other than Tennessee where the data on this many log structures have been analyzed in this way (Bishir 1990; Montell and Morse 1976; Wilson 1975).

OH, THE PLACES I'VE BEEN AND THE THINGS I'VE SEEN

The fieldwork involved in tracking down historic buildings has required more miles of travel than I can count. It has taken me to Mountain City, Shouns, Surgoinsville, Church Hill, Chuckey, Limestone, Thorn Hill, Puncheon Camp, Washburn, Powder Springs, Joppa, Sharp's Chapel, Lick Skillit, Hickory Star, Hickory Hollow, English Mountain, Ellijoy, Marble Springs, Wartburg, Sunbright, Allerdt, Rugby, Pall Mall, Frogge, Celina, Lewisburg, and Pulaski. I have been to counties named Polk, Bradley, Meigs, Rhea, Loudon, Knox, Blount, Sevier, Cocke, Union, Grainger, Hawkins, Hancock, Greene, Washington, Sullivan, and Johnson in eastern Tennessee's Ridge and Valley Province. On the Cumberland Plateau to the west, I have been to Morgan, Scott, Fentress, Overton, and Cumberland counties. On the Eastern Highland Rim, I explored Clay, Jackson, White, Dekalb, Putnam, Macon, and other counties. Nearing the Nashville Basin are Maury, Marshall, Giles, and

Lincoln counties, not to mention Davidson County, the home of Nashville proper. I have been to the rivers—Watauga, Holston, Clinch, Nolichuckey, French Broad, Pigeon, Little Pigeon, Little, Little Tennessee (Tellico), Hiwassee, Ocoee, Cumberland, Harpeth, Duck, Stones, Wolf, and Calfkiller, among others. I have seen towns and communities with classical names: Athens, Sparta, Carthage, Castalian Springs. I have traveled to Four Mile Creek, Six Mile Creek, and Nine Mile Creek, all in Blount county, and to Ten Mile Creek in Knox County. I have explored Shady Valley, Cades Cove, Tuckaleechee Cove, Wears Cove, Jones Cove, Richardson Cove, Grassy Cove, Colditz Cove, Carter Valley, Stanley Valley, Hickory Valley, and Red Boiling Springs. I've been to Crab Orchard and Ozone and to log churches called Okolona and Old Union. Gristmills give roads names like Robinson Mill, Mahoney Mill, Butler's Mill, and White's Mill. East Tennessee has dozens of late-eighteenth-century places with the word "station" attached to important, once-fortified farms: Shields Station, Gillespies Station, Cavetts Station, Campbells Station, Tipton Station, Singleton Station, Misers Station, and Ish Station. In the Nashville Basin, an old settled region dating from 1780, station names applied to Mansker, Eaton, Bledsoe, Robertson, Donelson, Hall, Brown, Buchanan, and others. A few of these survive on the landscape. The origins of names like Sam Houston Schoolhouse Road, Roberts Schoolhouse Road, Blowing Cave Road, Davy Crockett Road, and Needmore are obvious. Cultural hints of Germans appear in Hohenwald, Mosheim, and Dutch (which is really a corruption of *Deutsche*), as in Dutch Valley, Dutchtown, Dutch Bottoms, and Old Dutch Settlement. The Swiss settled Gruetli and Laager in Grundy County on the Cumberland Plateau. Don't be misled by place names like Lafayette, Monterey, Milan, Cardiff, and Lenoir City into thinking them exotic or Old World. While interesting from a local landscape point of view, these European-sounding places are still very much of Tennessee. Store signs can be catchy, like the M&M Little Giant Market in Carter Valley in Hawkins County, Old Drunks Used Cars in Cocke County northeast of Knoxville, and Bad Habits, a beer and tobacco establishment on Highway 31A near Pulaski in Giles County. Each place reflects the cultural uniqueness of this part of the country.

Respecting that cultural uniqueness is a crucial part of fieldwork. Let's say you are out in the field in rural Tennessee driving along small, winding country roads, possibly like those that James Taylor or John Denver sang about. You need to know how to wave. If you are meeting another vehicle and the driver is an old man, he may touch the brim of his hat and/or nod. You do the same or just give a miniscule wave with the fingers. If the driver is between 30 and 50 years old, he might wave with just a couple of fingers lifted from the steering wheel. You should do the same. Anybody under 25 will not likely wave at all. So don't bother to wave

Upper East Tennessee's Carter Valley and Stanley Valley (pictured here in March 2005) in Hawkins County are remarkably scenic rural landscapes and part of the old Watauga settlements (see chapter 2).

at them because they won't understand and might be suspicious of you. Never, never, never wave at a woman, no matter whether she is driving a car or truck or tractor, or just standing out in the yard. It is bad form and simply not done. On numbered state and busy federal highways, you can save your energy by not waving at all because nobody waves or greets one another in this way there. It is on small, winding, narrow county roads where the proper, mannerly wave becomes essential.

In a popular image of Appalachian life, a mountaineer responds to some flatland intruder by waving a gun and shooing him off the place. I must say that I've never had a gun pulled on me by someone who wasn't a relative. But that's another story from my wife's side of the family. Anyway, at one site in 1978 in Grainger County, I spied the owner with a pistol sticking out of his back pocket. I asked him why he carried a gun, and he explained that there had been several burglaries in the area and that he was just being prepared. I told him to just keep it in his pants because my fellow surveyor, John Morgan, and I meant no harm. We continued to survey his place and hundreds more that summer without incident.

Fieldwork can be fun and a bit scary. In April 2006, Chris Underwood and the author cautiously checked the Meek Williams site on English Mountain in Sevier County (see chapter 5).

Working in out-of-the-way places can have some real hazards, however, and in the field, I've seen some sure signs that say, "Don't go there." On May 25, 2005, I worked a Tennessee county (which I will not directly identify) that had *all* of the following characteristics: unnamed and unmarked one-lane gravel roads, hand-painted signs that said "no trespas," rooster enclosures with crowing fighting cocks inside, primer-painted cars (gray), primer-painted trailers (also gray), derelict trailers, trailers for rent, and—I'm not making this up—a road sign announcing "Doublewide Lane." Can you guess which Tennessee county this was? Was it Cocke in East Tennessee, Grundy on the Cumberland Plateau, Macon on the northern Highland Rim in Middle Tennessee, or Giles in the southwestern corner of the Nashville Basin and on the western Highland Rim? It could have been any one or all of them.

Animals can be sure clues, too. In addition to fighting cocks, one might see recently abandoned puppies, feral dogs, and rottweilers and pit bulls on logging chains. On the Walden's Ridge part of the Cumberland Plateau between Dayton and Pikeville, two huge, ferocious Rhodesian ridgebacks chased me. The dogs were serious because the hair on their backs stood straight up.

News reports about methamphetamine labs are also alarming. So, in fear, I have chosen to avoid certain locales. Scary, dangerous, crazy, toxic, and explosive are the traits of both meth making and meth addicts. I've been lucky or blessed because I haven't encountered a meth lab or meth user yet.

SURVEYING HISTORIC BUILDINGS

I've already mentioned the project that was behind all this fieldwork, but let's look at it a little more closely. Beginning in the 1970s, the Tennessee Historical Commission began a systematic survey on a county-by-county basis to inventory all historic buildings and structures that were 50 years old or older in Tennessee. The purpose of this ambitious survey was to compile a comprehensive inventory from which to identify potential structures for possible inclusion on the National Register of Historic Places. Contracts were let to survey teams from universities, high schools, and others. In 1978, my team conducted the first survey, beginning with Grainger County. I was the principal investigator, and my team comprised graduate students John Morgan, Joy Medford, and Stan Guffey. The next year we added graduate students Vince Ambrosia and Neil Cyganiak to survey Union County, Tennessee. For several years thereafter, Morgan, Medford, Ashby Lynch, and others surveyed Morgan and Blount counties. In recent years, John Morgan, who is now a professor at Emory and Henry College in Virginia, and his students have surveyed Johnson and Hawkins counties, among others in Upper East Tennessee. Survey teams at Tennessee Tech in Cookeville led by Calvin Dickinson, Michael Birdwell, and Homer Kemp surveyed 12 counties on the Cumberland Plateau (see Dickinson, Birdwell, and Kemp 2002). Across the state, Tennessee Historical Commission personnel, local county historians, and college and high school teachers and their students also did survey work on Tennessee's historic structures.

FIELDWORK, PHASE I

The methods and techniques for historic-building surveys require observant people with a lot of time. You must have a good field car to drive on all drivable county roads. Take either an old, beat-up car or, preferably, a four-wheel-drive vehicle. Don't drive your shiny new sports car because scratches, dents, dings, dust, and "gravel rash" come with the territory. Once I had to have my personal car, a blue 1972 Ford Torino, pulled out of a deep ditch by a farmer's John Deere tractor. Two other fellows on our field team did me one better. When they drove a University of Tennessee motor-pool car, a rickety white Ford Maverick, into a ditch, it required a farmer's mule to extract it.

Our field teams have required topographic maps of the county at 1:24,000 scale and two high-quality 35mm cameras with wide-angle lenses, one for black-and-white prints and one for color slides. (In more recent years, digital cameras have been used.) There is also a printed field form to be filled out for each structure. Starting at one end of the county, we drive until we see the first candidate

Any structure 50 years old or older is a candidate for historic buildings surveys, even the remains of this dogtrot house in Warren County. (Courtesy of the Tennessee Historical Commission.)

structure estimated to be at least 50 years old. We assign it a number, in this case number 1, write that number on the topographic map, draw a circle around the structure on the map, take photographs of the building from the corners both front and rear so as to include all building sides from two angles, and fill out the field form. On a good day, we might survey 10 or even 20 properties. There may be as few as 200 or as many as several thousand structures in a single county survey. The hours are long; the pay is low; the heat, humidity, and dust are uncomfortable. After a couple of months, boredom sets in. Fatigue, chiggers, ticks, poison ivy, snakes, and mean dogs are just some of the problems encountered. The work is rewarding, however, and as you will see in this book, it seems to be worth the effort.

DATA IN NASHVILLE

At the completion of a field survey, the county's field data are sent to Nashville and processed at the Tennessee Historical Commission. Data are microfilmed and archived at the state archives. Topographic maps are digitized, and building locations are recorded in latitude and longitude and in Universal Transverse Mercator (UTM) coordinates. Data from field forms are entered into a computer so that the researcher can query the data set and retrieve information. Since I am searching for log buildings, I enter key words like "log(s)" or "hewn timber(s)." The result is a list of buildings to which the key words apply. If I am lucky, the county in question will have data on the presence of log buildings, the current and past owner's names, an estimated age of the structure, a brief description of architectural features, and the latitude and longitude or UTM coordinates.

I have my own methods for using the data in Nashville. I examine the printed lists and arrange them in numerical order. Interestingly enough, what is for me pertinent data—building type, notch type, and timber type—is often not entered on field forms by other surveyors; and for the few that contain such information, the interpretations may have errors. So, I must examine the photographs for each numbered log structure in a given county's collection. Analyzing each photograph, I determine the building type (e.g., saddlebag house), the log notch type (e.g., half-dovetail), timber type (e.g., oak), condition, and general age. I also scan photographs of some of the better structures that might be worth a field inspection at a later time.

BACK IN KNOXVILLE

After working for a week at a time in Nashville, I return home to compile county data into spreadsheets and begin to analyze patterns and map concentrations by county, as well as determine percentages of the frequency of structure types. Next, I attempt to locate the best representative structures in the field, guided there by the UTM or latitude and longitude coordinates. Suppose I see a really interesting structure in the collection. I already have a scan of it so I make a note of its field number, such as BT1, which is Blount County's property number 1.

I now have two ways of working up this next step. The most accurate method is to enter the coordinates into a good handheld Global Positioning System (GPS) receiver. This device allows me to enter the coordinates in the same way I would while taking a waypoint in the field. By creating a waypoint, I can now identify the property by its county number, such as BT1, enter the UTM or latitude and longitude coordinates in the next box, then enter a description of the structure, such as "I-house, V notched." Next, I view a close-up map of the site displayed in the GPS unit; then I plot the structure/site location on a paper map in DeLorme's *Tennessee Atlas and Gazetteer* (2001).

Another way is to access the Internet, pull up the website for "mytopo.com," and enter the property's coordinates in the spaces provided for searching map locations. The website displays the topographic map of the area at 1:24,000 scale, with the site of interest marked with a red cross. Next, using the *Tennessee Atlas and Gazetteer*, I plot the location of my interest building on the paper map by eyeballing the screen map from "mytopo."

Another office activity is to make a digital photographic contact sheet of the select scanned images for a county. Adobe Photoshop Elements® has an extremely useful program for making such sheets. The contact sheet contains pictures of every image I have scanned; it also has each image identified by the discrete building number (e.g., BT1). This gives me an index of the scanned photos of log buildings in a given county. It also provides me with a visual reference guide for the next phase of fieldwork.

FIELDWORK, PHASE II

After plotting several log buildings, I am now ready to check on the presence or absence of selected structures. Armed with maps, contact sheets, cameras, a tape measure, and a GPS unit, I proceed to the field. The GPS and maps help navigate me to a structure site. I press the GPS's "go to" button to enter its data section. The GPS knows where I am located at all times, so it now directs me to the house site with a directional link between me and the site indicated as a straight line, or "as the crow flies."

At last I am at the property site, where I can photograph and verify the condition of the structure. The updated photography is now digital and can be processed in color or black and white on an office computer and printer. For example, in southern Jefferson County near the Sevier County line, I have rediscovered an impressive, photogenic single-pen house that has seen better days. Identified as the Whaley Place, the house has half-dovetail notches on yellow poplar logs. In spite of acute weathering and deterioration, the little single-pen is being protected and carefully watched by its owners. It would be nice if more people in our state were consciously protecting the few log structures remaining on the landscape; better yet would be professional restorations of many of the more vulnerable buildings such as this one.

Sadly, many structures are gone, or else the location data are in error or are incomplete. Not all properties featured in this book have been field-checked since the date they were originally surveyed. Some of the featured properties recently field-checked and photographed no longer survive. Furthermore, I occasionally find undocumented log structures in the field by accident, buildings that for some reason were not caught in the formal Tennessee Historical Commission's survey. Still, this kind of fieldwork is fun, it gets me out of the office, and it connects me to the landscape and its people.

HOW OLD IS THIS LOG BUILDING?

When I ask folks in the field about the age of a log structure, the popular answers I get are: "built before the Civil War" or "a hundred years old." Or someone might say, "This house was around these parts when Tennessee was still North Carolina," meaning before 1796. For some reason, people often like to exaggerate a building's age. Their tales are like a fish story in which the fish gets bigger with each telling. And so, with log buildings, the more they tell the story, the older the

The author rediscovered this single-pen house in Jefferson County using map coordinates and a GPS in 2005.

Discovering Folk Architecture

building becomes. I cannot always accept such answers as accurate, so I rely on other means for dating log buildings. Calculating a building's approximate age is difficult, and my field experience in Appalachia has helped me tremendously, enabling me to make educated guesses based on my knowledge of the landscape and the confirmed dates of a few select buildings I already know well. If the logs are yellow poplar or oak and are wider than 12 inches, for example, then I know that the structure is probably old, predating 1880 and possibly even 1840. If the timber is a pine species and left in the round, not hewn, it is considered a younger property. The corner notches may also point to age. A pattern of V notches or full-dovetail notches indicates a house considerably older than one with saddle or saddle-V notches. Half-dovetail notches often fall somewhere in between. These buildings may be younger than those with V and full-dovetail notches but are older than buildings with saddle and saddle-V notches. Thus, saddle notches found on round pine logs tell me that the house was probably built after 1880 and is likely to have been built between 1930 and 1940—and possibly as late as the 1950s. Saw marks can help. Straight-line saw marks indicate crosscut sawing, a method predating the steam-operated sawmills that emerged in the 1870s and '80s. Circular or arc marks from a circular saw tell me the wood was worked at a sawmill no earlier than the 1870s and more likely in the 1880–1930 period or later. A chimney may aid diagnosis as well. Stone chimneys are usually older than brick ones; stovepipes and cinderblock chimneys are certainly younger. Chimney replacements can lead to confusion, however, so one has to be careful in dating a house by the chimney alone.

    While inspecting a site, I often search for the old family name or the old owner's full name. Thus, another source of information about a building's age comes from analyzing a nearby family cemetery to match the former occupant's name with the property. Let's say a man named Jacob Frye (a fictional name) owned the place. In the family cemetery, I locate Jacob's gravestone and learn that he was born in 1822 and died in 1884. If he constructed the place at the age of 20, the structure could have been built around 1842. It is entirely possible that he may have built it in his teens but not likely before he was 15. Or Jacob could have built it while in his 30s, perhaps his 40s, but it is less likely that he did so after the age of 60. So, for the Frye place, we have a range of years between 1842 and 1884 based on the working lifetime of its initial owner. We don't want to estimate too late because during the Civil War years, 1861–65, it's possible that Jacob Frye was not there to build a log house but was fighting in the war instead. If I lean toward the 1842 mark, when Frye was 20, the 1842–52 bracket is a bit more plausible. Since the wood is yellow poplar and displays V notches, I am thinking that this is an old place. By now, I am definitely leaning toward 1842 and certainly no later than 1860 for this two-pen saddlebag house (Rehder 2004, 92–93).

DENDROCHRONOLOGY

The search described above is one that I have repeated in the field and with courthouse records and archives. But another way to date log buildings is through dendrochronology, the science of using tree rings to study climatic variability, as well as to determine the age of wooden objects, in this case log structures. Many of us remember from childhood counting the tree rings on a stump in the forest to calculate the age of a tree at the time it was cut. Dendrochronology is far more scientific and combines fieldwork and laboratory research. At the University of Tennessee, cores taken from trees or timbers are analyzed in the Laboratory for Tree Ring Science using sophisticated computer techniques to compare rings from our sites with a known master chronology. I have worked in this way with geography faculty colleague Henri Grissino-Mayer and former and present graduate students Bill Reding, David Mann, Chris Underwood, and Saskia van der Gevel. Using techniques of dendrochronology, Reding and Mann determined the dates for five log buildings in East Tennessee. Reding examined four log buildings with one each from the contiguous counties of Union, Grainger, Jefferson, and Hamblin. Tennessee Historical Commission teams had surveyed the buildings in the late 1970s. I was the principal investigator on the Grainger and Union County surveys in 1978 and 1979. In 2001, Reding took core samples in the logs of the structures and, with dendrochronology, established confirmed dates for when the trees were cut. He discovered that a Union County blacksmith shop built of yellow poplar logs using half-dovetail notches had a dendrochronology date of 1793. The earlier surveyor's estimate of 1790 that John

Dendrochronology, the science of tree-ring dating, often involves drilling core samples with a hollow saw. Cores are matched to known tree-ring records in the Laboratory for Tree Ring Science at the University of Tennessee to determine the year when the tree was cut.

Discovering Folk Architecture

This log house in Hamblen County, featuring V notches on yellow poplar logs, was dated to 1812 with dendrochronology analysis by William M. Reding in 2002.

Morgan and I had made was based on interviews and intuitive fieldwork. In Grainger County, a smokehouse built with yellow poplar logs and half-dovetail notches was dated to 1860 from dendrochronology; Morgan and I had estimated the date at 1850. Reding's dendrochronology determined a date of 1812 for a log I-house constructed of yellow poplar logs and V notches in Hamblin County; the earlier surveyors' estimate was 1815. In Jefferson County, another I-house built with half-dovetailed yellow poplar logs (a structure now in complete ruin) had a dendrochronology date of 1827; the surveyor's estimate was 1835 (Reding 2002, 41–51). I am pleased that our surveyors' estimates came so close to the dates verified by dendrochronology. I am especially gratified that we now have an accurate method for determining the age of log structures found virtually anywhere in the region (Rehder 2004, 94).

The benefits of dendrochronology were also evident in dating an unusual log building in Cocke County. Built of red oak timbers with half-dovetailed notches, it was known as the "Swaggerty Blockhouse." A blockhouse was an early fortified log building that served as a corner unit in a military fort; in some cases, it was a stand-alone fortified house. A blockhouse often represented the first effective settlement phase in a region. (Fort Marr, located in Polk County, is perhaps the last-known genuine blockhouse in Tennessee; it is popularly thought to have been built in 1814.)

At the Swaggerty building in Cocke County, there is a large metal historical marker stating that it was built by a James Swaggerty around 1787 for protection from Indians. With the present owner's permission, David Mann cored the logs, took 37 samples, and with dendrochronology techniques came up with a date of 1860 for the structure—more than seven decades later than the marker date. Then, using archaeological methods and an analysis of materials excavated from 42 shovel test pits on the site to verify his findings from dendrochronology, Mann arrived at average dates of 1860 for nails and 1864 for glass shards on the site. Far from being a fortification against Indian attacks during the early settlement period, the "Swaggerty Blockhouse" turned out to be a cantilevered springhouse and hog enclosure built by farmer Jacob Stephens in 1860 (Mann 2002, 88–92; Rehder 2004, 94–95; Mann, Grissino-Mayer, Faulkner, Rehder 2009).

Using dendrochronology and archaeological techniques, David Mann determined that the "Swaggerty Blockhouse" (Cocke County) was actually built in the 1860s, not 1787 as was popularly thought.

Discovering Folk Architecture

Since 2002, more dendrochronology research on log architecture in Tennessee has been conducted at several sites. At the Hermitage, Andrew Jackson's plantation northeast of Nashville, a slave dwelling called Alfred's cabin has a confirmed date of 1843, two years before Andrew Jackson died (Grissino-Mayer 2006). The logs are of eastern red cedar, unusual trees for most of Tennessee but a common species in the limestone soils of the Nashville Basin.

Marble Springs, John Sevier's plantation south of Knoxville, has two buildings, the first of which is believed to be the site of the original Sevier single-pen house. A frontiersman, military and political leader, and state hero, Sevier (1745–1815) had occupied the site sometime between 1792 and 1815 (West 1995, 71–72). The structure had been restored with many younger pine logs, but the oldest oak logs there have a date of 1834–35. The second structure at Marble Springs, described in chapter 5 as "the house that moved" from west Knoxville in 1988, has dendrochronology dates of 1826–27 (Grissino-Mayer, Jan. 24, 2007).

In Upper East Tennessee is a site called Rocky Mount, where the first territorial capital had been established by Gov. William Blount (1749–1800) for 1790–92. The original log-building complex was thought to have been constructed in 1770–72. However, dendrochronological research indicates a date between 1827 and 1830 (Grissino-Mayer and van de Gevel 2007).

So, what's going on? We know that trees don't lie. Buildings are restored with newer, younger logs; some buildings are moved from one site to another. The changes may not be recorded, so subsequent owners and historians are led to believe that the structure's logs are the *original* ones and date to a specific earlier time. At the Rocky Mount site, someone apparently reconstructed the site with logs cut in the years 1827–30, or else the site is incorrectly identified on the landscape (Grissino-Mayer and van de Gevel 2007). Such mistaken identities have happened elsewhere in America. In spite of what courthouse deeds might say about land ownership, events such as site restorations, renovations, and even relocated roads and tracks are not always recorded. Thus, tree rings remain our best source for determining the date when logs were cut for a building.

TENNESSEE DISCOVERIES

I have been working with historical buildings survey data collected throughout the state since 1977, and I already have data on more than 4,200 log structures. However, almost every time I go out in the field, I discover a log structure that did not appear in the original survey data. Throughout all of this, I have had interesting encounters with people, places, and things. I'll talk a little about some of those here and include other stories in later chapters. Some of my discoveries came as unexpected log-structure surprises; some arrived with no building in sight.

PRIVATE INVESTIGATOR?

In late January 2005, I was working in Middle Tennessee, specifically in White County south of Sparta (a home of bluegrass music legend Lester Flatt). Lying just east of Milksick Mountain, the area is a beautiful limestone valley called Hickory Valley. I had come into the area from the west off highway TN 111 on Old Union Road. Upon entering the valley proper, I was immediately struck by an open pastoral setting with hundreds of cows and punctuated everywhere by modern silos and dairy barns. The scene was so striking that I had to stop in the middle of this quiet country road and take pictures.

As I was about to leave, I looked up to my right and saw two men in their 20s at a small white house. I politely waved as I drove past them and thought nothing more about it. My mission here was to find a specific log structure, WH16, and I was nearing the spot where it was supposed to be located. My field photo taken in 1983 showed it to be a small but rather elegant, certainly photogenic single-pen log house in an open field. GPS in hand, I followed the track out to the site but to no avail. The house was missing. I saw nothing to indicate that the house was anywhere around, so I proceeded to a small cemetery road and backed in my Ford Explorer. Here I could regroup, check my maps, consult the GPS, and take a swig of soda.

A few minutes later, a maroon car pulled up, and out jumped the two fellows from the house a ways back. The bearded one spoke first: "Whatcha doin takin' pitchers back thar?" I explained that I was with UT (out here it is better just to use the initials than to declare, "University of Tennessee") and that I was doing work on log buildings in the area. Still bothered, the bearded one explained that his buddy had been in court that very day as part of a child-custody battle, and they thought that I was "some kinda private investigator" snooping around his place. I assured him that I was no such thing and showed him the 1983 contact photograph of WH16 and asked if he had ever seen it. No, neither he nor his anxious buddy had ever seen the long-lost log house. Satisfied that I meant no harm, they left. And, happily, so did I.

Minutes later and a couple of miles down Hickory Valley Road, I was heading back to Sparta another way. I stopped to photograph an old barn with some log cribs under it. I couldn't tell much about the structure because of the weatherboarding, but it looked like it might be either a four-crib or transverse-crib barn. It didn't appear to be a cantilever barn, however. As I was about to leave, a black pickup truck with two different fellows stopped to check on me. The driver asked if I was having car trouble. I said that my truck was okay and that I was on my way back to Sparta. Whew, another close call.

What was going on here? I think I can explain. In rural areas where farming is still practiced full time, residents are far more observant of outsiders.

Discovering Folk Architecture

Full-time farmers work and watch their land, property, crops, and cattle much more diligently and protectively than do rural non-farm folks. Non-farm rural residents commute to work in town and then return at quitting time to have supper, watch some TV, and go to bed. They are not always in the habit of watching and protecting their property and surroundings in the same manner or with the same degree of suspicion as full-time farm folk.

NAKANAWA AND A 12-SIDED LOG BUILDING

The Cumberland Plateau region has an unusual heritage of human habitation. Sparsely settled over much of its history, the region has remained a forested wilderness. Its sandstone caprock surface has yielded little in the way of agriculture. Moreover, lacking adequate surface water and access, the region was unattractive to Native American Cherokees as well as pioneer settlers of European descent. So, how have people used the lands of the Cumberland Plateau? Aside from early and limited coal-mining activity and a more extensive logging in hardwoods and managed softwoods for the pulp and paper industry, the region has become a place for recreation in the form of summer camps, state parks, and retirement communities.

Nakanawa is a summer camp for girls aged 8 to 17. It is located near Mayland, 12 miles west of Crossville in Cumberland County. You reach it by taking Interstate 40 Exit 301, about 85 miles west of Knoxville and 100 miles east of Nashville. The private camp has been operating continuously since 1920, and some of its buildings actually date from 1919.

In my Cumberland County survey data, I had noticed an unusual multisided log structure, number CU877. I first thought it might be an octagon; but I was fairly certain that it was odd, old, and worth investigating. On Friday, February 4, 2005, my old green Explorer bounced me along the correct roads as I followed my trusty GPS. Tracing the trail like a bloodhound, the GPS took me straight to the Nakanawa Camp but not directly to the log building. Thinking that the odd structure might be missing, I turned the Explorer around, something I'm pretty good at doing in the middle of a country road or in someone's driveway. All the while, a big black Labrador retriever was barking loudly and checking my vehicle as I slowly retreated from the camp. Out of the corner of my eye, I saw a woman walking out to the road. I stopped, introduced myself, and told her about my work on log buildings. The woman was Ann Perron, owner of the camp since 1981; and she said that the multisided log building was indeed still on site, giving me permission to look it over and photograph it. She explained that the building was not octagonal but actually had 12 sides. It was built in 1919 as one of the first build-

The 12-sided "Wigwam" was built in 1919 at Camp Nakanawa, a girls' summer camp west of Crossville in Cumberland County.

ings in the camp. The complex had been a girls' camp since its founding in 1920 by Col. L. L. Rice, who ran the camp until 1947.

The photographs I took reveal a 12-sided, nearly circular, "wigwam-like" log structure that is actually named "The Wigwam." The round logs are of very small diameter and consist of pine, red oak, and even some persimmon and dogwood species. Held together with bolts instead of corner notches, the structure is surprisingly sturdy and in very good condition. Mrs. Perron said that the original cement chinking had begun to crumble, so a commercial log-house company was hired to rechink the structure with Permachink®. This product is used in the commercial log-structures business because it has some flexibility when the weather changes. She also said that the Crab Orchard sandstone chimney was original but that the roof had been replaced with a tin one. I thanked Ann Perron for her time and information, waved at her husband, Pepe, who was perched on a tractor, saluted the old black Lab, and went on my way. With fieldwork like this, you couldn't have a much better day.

Discovering Folk Architecture

SEARCHING FOR A MUD-AND-STICK CHIMNEY

I was heading up to Hawkins County, Tennessee, on March 4, 2005. This sparkling clear day was cold and windy but a good field day. Winter is the best time for fieldwork because the leaves are off the trees, allowing you to see entire buildings. When spring and summer arrive, the leaves obscure both vision and photography. Moreover, as the weather warms up, ticks, chiggers, and snakes become active and pose real problems.

I had gone to Hawkins County to find a deteriorating house, HW692, that still had a mud-and-stick chimney when John Morgan surveyed it in 1987. I speedily took I-81 to TN 70. Going west, I passed through a narrow gap through a ridge called Piney Mountain and proceeded to Kite Road, where my little GPS told me to turn right. I headed northeast along the road, did a zig, and took Webster Valley Road several country miles farther, coming to a stop sign. The GPS was only line of sight ("as the crow flies"), so I got my bearings and did a zag to take "Opossum Hollow Road." That was what the green road sign said, but don't you bet they really mean "possum holler" around here? It was a single-lane road (perhaps one-and-a-half lanes at best), once graveled but now macadamed with tar and crushed rock. Beneath a canopy of leafless deciduous trees, the sun-dappled trail followed a narrow creek strewn with brush, trash, and old tires. At one place was a whole set of four tires lying on the creek bank. A shack here, trailers there, some new clearings opening up, a lot for sale—these sights punctuated the peaceful drive through the glade. I went a bit farther and turned right on Honeycutt and left onto Long Bend Road and approached the log structure sites HW690 (a single-crib with gear shed), HW692 (my primary target, a saddlebag house with the mud-and-stick chimney), and HW696 (a newer log pole barn). Sad to say, only the small single-crib with gear shed remained on the landscape. Both the saddlebag house and pole barn were gone, and so with them went my hopes of finding an authentic log structure with that rare mud-and-stick chimney. As of 2011, I have yet to find one.

OTHER SITES

I keep running into houses and barns out on the landscape almost by accident. In the southwest corner of Clay County I turned off of TN 52 at Hermitage Springs and took Trace Creek Road to locate a rare log four-pen house identified as CY41. It being late when I found it, I had trouble getting a good photo but took pictures anyway. I was heading out of the county to make the long journey back home to Knoxville. The GPS was having a rare moment, not following any road pattern that corresponded to where I was. Not lost entirely but getting lost by the minute,

Authentic mud-and-stick chimneys, like this one in Hawkins County, are almost impossible to find because they either burned up during the early occupation of the structure or were soon replaced with limestone or brick chimneys. (Courtesy of the Tennessee Historical Commission.)

I drove south to reach Bakertown Road. It turned in almost all directions: south, then east, then west. I wanted to go east but the road didn't go that way for long. At some point I rounded a curve and discovered a neat double-crib barn with an open drive-through. I numbered it CY001. The barn, featured as an example in chapter 4, had saddle-V notches on small round logs that appeared to be pine. The ends were sawn, indicating that it was not a very old structure. I estimated it to be from the 1940s—perhaps from the 1950s, but not any later. It certainly was not a nineteenth-century structure. The tin roof was in good condition, and the farm on which the barn stood was a well-maintained cattle operation.

There is an old saying: "A geographer never gets lost." For me that is quite untrue. I am always going somewhere only to become temporarily disoriented by

Discovering Folk Architecture

misreading or traveling off the map, or finding some other way of getting lost. So far, however, I have made it back home safe and sound.

In Putnam County, on TN 62 between Clark Range and Monterey, I photographed a transverse crib barn built with saddle-V notches on round oak logs. From all appearances, the barn had been well maintained, and it is possible that it may have been moved to the present site. This transverse-crib barn is the featured example in chapter 4.

The field, where the raw material for much of this book was found, is a place of continuous discovery and change. Log buildings seen one week are gone the next. Since the 1970s, the THC historic building surveys have been a rich blessing to me, a special way of discovering Tennessee's landscape heritage. Every place and every landscape has a history. In the next chapter, we will examine Tennessee's settlement history.

Chapter 2

Two Tennessee Hearths: A Settlement History

The total human history for any region and its culture is important. However, time and space preclude us from covering the Native American phases and early European exploration periods for our brief look at Tennessee. So, let's begin at the time of first effective European settlement for two hearths in the region. It is a time frame that begins around 1768–69 for the first hearth, the Watauga Settlements in Upper East Tennessee in the northeastern part of the state. Then, beginning in 1780, a second hearth originally called the Cumberland Settlements emerged in Middle Tennessee in the Nashville vicinity. But before we examine these two culturally important hearths, we should look at Tennessee's place within a regional, cultural context. How, we may ask, does Tennessee fit in with the rest of the South?

THE CULTURAL CONTEXT OF THE SOUTH

Tennessee occupies a place in U.S. geography that shares several cultural, economic, and physical regions. The state belongs to two large culture regions called the Upland South and the Lowland South. The Upland South, the much larger of the two, covers a widespread part of the South with Southern Appalachia as its core. The Upland South in the broadest sense is a culture region based on its identification with a Scotch-Irish heritage (Newton 1974, 150–53), even though German and English groups are well represented. It is "upland" owing to the physical highland core in Southern Appalachia. It is certainly "South" by virtue of its geographic location, but economic and social roots blur the region's identity. Historically, the Upland South has been characterized by small subsistence farms, very few slaves during the pre–Civil War era, and land with steeper slopes and higher elevations (Jordan-Bychkov 2003, 1–22).

The Lowland South is characterized by level to gently rolling landscapes that go from sea level to elevations of 500 to 1,000 feet. The region's historical identity comes from a plantation economy based on tobacco, rice, cotton, and sugarcane and supported by slave labor during the antebellum period. As a result, large numbers of African Americans are identified with the Lowland or Deep South. Both the Upland South and much of the Lowland South have been English-speaking by virtue of their Scotch-Irish and English heritages.

The Upland South also may be defined by cultural absences. Excluded, for example, is French Louisiana, a triangularly shaped culture region based on French colonial Creoles and Cajuns in southern Louisiana. We also exclude the English Tidewater, a very narrow strip of coastal culture that extends from southeastern Virginia to south coastal Georgia. The Tidewater is a Low Country, English colonial, plantation-based region.

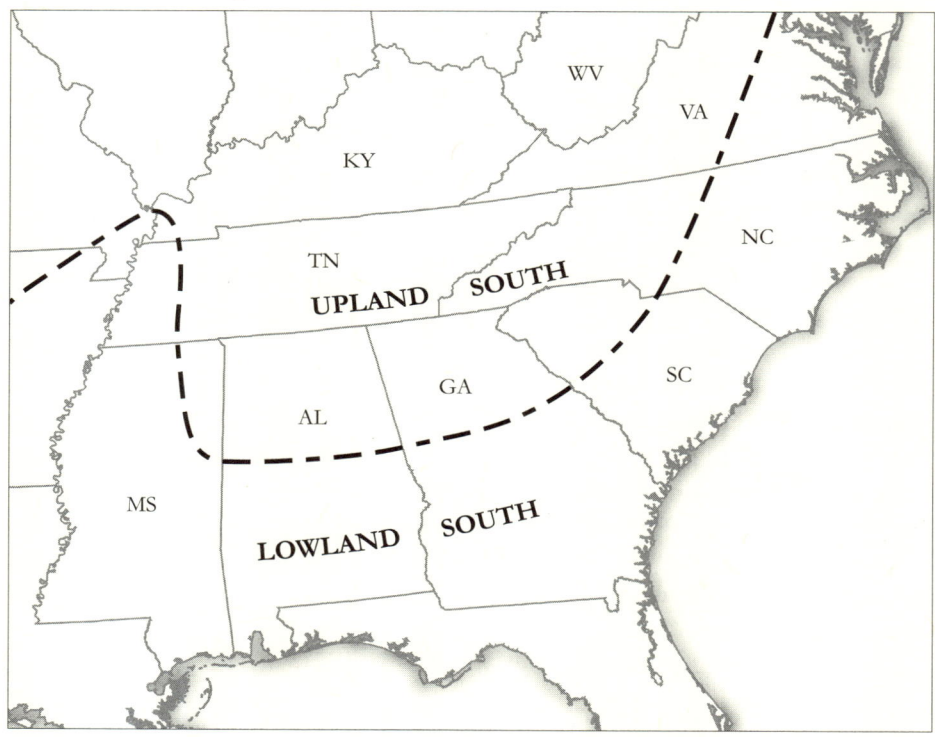

The Upland South and Lowland South regions of the United States.

While both French Louisiana and the English Tidewater are not part of the Upland South, they are integral to the Lowland South. Southern Florida, southern in latitude but far from southern culture, is excluded from all "Souths." Southern Florida's present-day cosmopolitan cultures of Cubans, Haitians, and other Latin Americans, along with retirees from northern regions of the United States, speak loudly and clearly of the unique identity of this part of the country (Rehder 1999, 51–55; Rehder 2004, 53).

TENNESSEE'S UPLAND AND LOWLAND SOUTH

About 80 percent of Tennessee lies in the Upland South, which includes East and Middle Tennessee. The other 20 percent lies in the Lowland South, located in the western part of the state. Little wonder that Tennessee has the unique distinction of being officially described as the Three States of Tennessee: East, Middle, and West. The three "states" are so well recognized that Tennessee's flag bears three white stars representing the three grand divisions. (The map opposite page 1 shows these divisions.)

Another way to describe Tennessee is in the context of Appalachia. About one half of Tennessee is in Southern Appalachia proper, the core region and heart of the Upland South. East Tennessee, comprising physical landform regions called the Blue Ridge Province and the Ridge and Valley Province, is entirely in Southern Appalachia. Middle Tennessee is centered on the Nashville Basin but includes the nearby upland landform regions of the Cumberland Plateau and surrounding rim country called the Eastern Highland Rim and the Western Highland Rim. However, only the eastern portions of Middle Tennessee, comprising the Cumberland Plateau and the Eastern Highland Rim, belong to Southern Appalachia. The Nashville Basin, at the center of Middle Tennessee, is still in the Upland South but is west of and out of Appalachia. In other words, all of Middle Tennessee is in the Upland South, but only its eastern parts are considered Appalachian.

Some people believe that the rich plantation lands surrounding Nashville and its near twin, the Kentucky Bluegrass Basin, could be considered part of the Lowland South because of their slave-based plantation economies during the early nineteenth century. But others argue that their cultural links to the Upland South exclude them from a Lowland South identity, whatever their economic histories.

Tennessee's undisputed piece of the Lowland South is a small area in West Tennessee with a special focus on Memphis in southwestern Tennessee. West Tennessee is the territory between the Mississippi River and the Tennessee River on its northerly flow towards Kentucky. The area is a part of a long finger of an

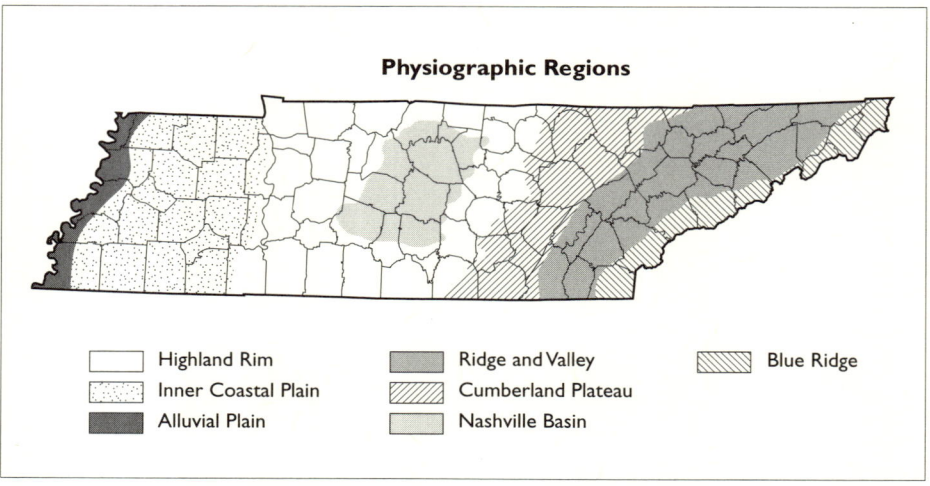

The physiographic regions of Tennessee. From left to right (west to east), they are the Alluvial Plain, Inner Coastal Plain, Highland Rim, Nashville Basin (shaded area within Highland Rim), Cumberland Plateau, Ridge and Valley, and Blue Ridge.

ancient coastal plain that extended up the Lower Mississippi River Valley. It is lowland for topographic, alluvial floodplain reasons, and it is lowland by cultural standards as well. A well-developed plantation economy, based on cotton with Anglo planters as the primary culture bearers, found its way into this flat part of Tennessee. Thus, the westernmost part along the Mississippi River and the southwestern corner around Memphis are considered physically and culturally part of the Lowland South.

As a place for settlers, Tennessee's natural landscapes provided a forested region of mountains, ridges, valleys, plateaus, and plains, with a complex geology and soils history. There were numerous clear streams but few natural lakes. The land offered abundant water, useful woodlands, selectively rich soils, and a moderate climate with sunlight and rainfall suitable for mid-latitude agriculture. It also presented hardships in some areas with steep, rocky slopes, relatively poor soils, physical isolation, difficult transportation access, and occasionally harsh winters and hot, humid summers. Most of the earliest permanent settlement focused on the favorable soils and slopes adjacent to the Great Valley routes that the settlers followed in the Ridge and Valley region in East Tennessee. Likewise, early settlers in the Nashville Basin chose the rich limestone soils, springs, and salt licks there. Only later did settlement expand to extreme areas of lesser soil quality and steeper slopes. From this, we can perceive a natural landscape that allowed Tennessee's people to create a variety of cultural landscapes.

INITIAL OCCUPANCE AND FIRST EFFECTIVE SETTLEMENT

In the history of any human settlement, the recognition of the initial occupance of a place and first effective settlement are key concepts because they aid in understanding successive settlement layers (Kniffen 1965, 551; McIntire 1958; Zelinsky 1992, 13–14; Rehder 1999, 29–30, 61; Rehder 2004, 72–73). Initial occupance always marks the very first layer of human settlement. In a conceptual model based on the multilayered *tell* settlements of the ancient Middle East, a settlement may have several layers, but the very first layer is important to our understanding of site selection and how this initial layer relates to subsequent layers.

Conversely, the concept of first effective settlement recognizes layers but puts more emphasis on the *effectiveness* of a first layer and perhaps adjacent significant subsequent layers. If the first contact with the land was minimal, the concept allows for other layers to occur until an effective permanent settlement emerges. The earliest European contacts with Tennessee by explorers, long hunters, and military expeditions created virtually no permanent settlements. Rather, these groups made "touch-and-go" landings and left little or no lasting impression or evidence of permanent European settlement. When earnest European settlers arrived in Upper East Tennessee after 1768–69 to clear land and establish fortified farmsteads called stations, the first effective settlement was then realized. In late-eighteenth-century Tennessee, Scotch-Irish, German, and English settlers—people who put together settlement patterns that have endured for more than 200 years—created a first effective permanent layer of European settlement.

So, here is a land of unmatched beauty, a land with tall mountains, green trees, flat valleys, choice natural springs and streams, and good soils. Although the land was attractive to Europeans in the late eighteenth and early nineteenth centuries, physical and cultural barriers slowed the migration. Mountain barriers, lands claimed by other Europeans, and the presence of Cherokees and other Native Americans presented the main challenges. This third factor was particularly important during the 1674–1838 period, as sharp conflicts developed between Native Americans and the white newcomers.

Among those conflicts were differing views of land use and ownership. From the Cherokee perspective, people could use the land but did not clearly own it: land was like the clouds, rain, sunshine, and oxygen, elements of the earth that were shared but not owned. It was a system of usufruct rights that was at odds with European notions of ownership, which saw land as there for the taking, something to be possessed. Of course, it was only a matter of time before the European perspective won out, and the lands long occupied by Native Americans were taken over by incoming settlers.

EUROPEAN MIGRATIONS

The ethnic patterns of Southern Appalachia and Tennessee particularly embraced diverse European culture groups. Dominant were Scotch-Irish, German, and English groups that had a major impact on the development of folk landscapes in the region. Eighteenth-century German and Scotch-Irish settlers entered the Appalachian region and Tennessee from two eastern ports of entry: Philadelphia, Pennsylvania, and Charleston, South Carolina. Philadelphia was not only the earlier port but also the more important one: from there thousands of immigrants were funneled first towards the west and then down the southwesterly trend of the Ridge and Valley Province along the Great Valley. Traveling on an ancient pathway called the Great Philadelphia Wagon Road (also known as the Great Wagon Road) from southeastern Pennsylvania to Roanoke, Virginia, settlers gradually made their way southward. This old route later became US 11, and, more recently, parts of it are covered by Interstate 81. Near Roanoke

Blockhouses protected early settlers. Fort Marr (c. 1814) also became part of a stockade for holding Cherokees before the infamous "Trail of Tears" removal in 1837–38. This structure with half-dovetailed pine logs was moved from the Old Federal Road near the Tennessee-Georgia line to its present site in Benton next to the old Polk County Jail.

(earlier called Big Lick), the route divided, and an eastern branch took settlers to the North Carolina Piedmont area around Salem and from there to Salisbury and points southward, all the way to Augusta, Georgia, a British trading post founded in 1735. From Roanoke, the western branch, called the Wilderness Road, took settlers to southwestern Virginia, northeastern Tennessee, and then to the Cumberland Gap, where between 1775 and 1810 an estimated 300,000 people passed through this most important gateway to the West (Blethen and Wood 2001; Dickson 1966; Rouse 1995; Rehder 2004, 64–71).

Other immigrants from the British Isles, chiefly the English, Welsh, Irish, and Scots, entered Appalachia at various times and in relatively small numbers. The English, who had played a decisive role in initiating, occupying, and developing the Tidewater coastal region between southeastern Virginia and southeastern Georgia, kept their focus on the narrow coastal region that faced the Atlantic towards Mother Britain. Eventually, however, an upcountry British presence developed as eastern seaboard lands were taken up and as interior lands became available. Small but not insignificant groups such as African-Americans, Native Americans who remained in the East after the Indian removals (notably Cherokees, Shawnees, Creeks, and Chickasaws), and even the mysterious Melungeons all made their presence felt in Tennessee, creating a place of rich cultural diversity (Rehder 1992, 99; Kennedy 1997; Rehder 2004, 53–71).

THE WATAUGA HEARTH: UPPER EAST TENNESSEE 1768–1769

The Watauga River flows from western North Carolina into northeastern Tennessee, a region best known today as Upper East Tennessee. The river laboriously works its way through a deep gorge in the mountainous Blue Ridge Province before opening onto a broad valley in the Ridge and Valley Province in Tennessee. Here the Watauga joins the Holston River, and the two streams together formed a regional focus for settlers to gather in the late eighteenth century.

Beginning around 1768 or 1769, settlers entered this northeastern corner of Tennessee from two directions. One movement followed the east-to-west trend of the Watauga River with explorers such as Daniel Boone, John Sevier, and James Robertson leading settler groups from western North Carolina. Another, more important route came from the northeast and followed the trend of the Wilderness Road in the Great Valley along the Holston River in the Ridge and Valley Province. This route led all the way from southeastern Pennsylvania through western Maryland and Virginia to northeastern Tennessee. This Great Valley route became the more significant path because many more settlers and a greater variety of culture groups entered the region this way. Historian Samuel Cole Williams suggested that perhaps 80 percent of the early settlers to the Watauga area had arrived via this route, which comprised the Great Wagon and Wilderness roads mentioned above (Williams 1937; Dixon [1976], 5).

Ethnically, the area is thought to be heavily Scotch-Irish, but few factual sources can prove it because the First United States Census in 1790 failed to identify a specific category of people called *Scotch-Irish*. The census identified Scots, Irish, Welsh, and English but no Scotch-Irish, a term that came to be applied to American descendants of Scots who had migrated to northern Ireland during the 1600s. It was a term not in use during the late 1700s. Such is the dilemma of cultural identities (Rehder 2004, 53–57). For Watauga, the early settlement leaders represented various ethnicities: James Robertson was Scotch-Irish, John Sevier was French Huguenot, Evan Shelby was Welsh, William Bean was Highland Scot, and John Carter and Jacob Brown were English (Dixon [1976], 5).

Permanent settlement took root in four specific settlement areas. Whether they were land grants or purchases, each area had a leader, a person who had acquired property and had built a store that became a central place of social and economic activity. The North Holston settlement was located on the Holston River near the present-day city of Bristol, Tennessee/Virginia. Evan Shelby, described as a hard-drinking Welshman, established a store there and the settlement quickly expanded around it. A second area that became the chief Watauga Settlement was also called Sycamore Shoals. Located along the Watauga River, the settlement centered at what is today the city of Elizabethton. Watauga's early leaders here were William Bean and James Robertson. A Virginian named John Carter from Amherst, Virginia, established the third settlement called Carter's Valley, located to the west of the others. Carter arrived around 1770 or 1771, initially to trade with Cherokee hunting parties. Like others, Carter built a store that became the settlement's focus. The Carter Valley settlement encompassed the valleys of three streams: the Clinch River, the Holston River, and Beech Creek. Much of present-day Hawkins County was originally the Carter Valley settlement.

The fourth settlement, called the Nolichucky Settlement, was established by Jacob Brown, a South Carolina merchant and early leader who purchased two enormous tracts of land along the course of the Nolichucky River. Brown's Nolichucky Settlement was the southernmost of the four (Alderman 1970, 55; Dixon [1976], 4–11).

Collectively, these four settlements became a culturally important regional hearth known as the "Watauga Settlements." Fed by settlers from the Pennsylvania hearth of Germans and Scotch-Irish near Philadelphia, as well as settlers from Virginia, Maryland, and especially western North Carolina, the Watauga hearth became a tertiary settlement region. In 1784, realizing their unique level of cohesiveness, the people of the Watauga Settlements formed the "State of Franklin," a short-lived attempt at independence from North Carolina. The Wataugans may have had Scotch-Irish and German heritages, but they developed into an American frontier culture with a pioneer way of life. It was from the Watauga Settlements hearth, a "mother island" of sorts, that European settlers later diffused to points west and south in Tennessee and then to distant locales in Arkansas, Missouri, and Texas (Jordan-Bychkov 2003, 5–22).

A WATAUGA HEARTH LOG HOUSE

An excellent representative old log house site is found in Greene County near Chuckey on the right bank of the Nolichucky River. The Heinrich Ernst two-story log house is reported to have been built in 1784, and if true, that would make it one of Tennessee's oldest standing log houses (West 1995, 135–36). I call it the Heinrich Ernst place because a German settler of that name from North Carolina built it. However, you will see it identified in other sources as the Mauris-Earnest Fort House and also under the Anglicized name of the Henry Earnest place. This wonderful representation of early German log construction measures 30 feet wide by 21 feet deep. The oak logs are notched with the old-style V notch. The single chimney, built of rough-cut stone, has separate flues serving the two floors of the house. The house remains in good condition thanks to the stone cellar and foundation that prevent the sill logs from rotting, to the careful preservation by the Earnest (Ernst) family through the centuries, and to a listing in the National Register of Historic Places.

I first encountered the Ernst place while working with some Historic American Buildings Survey (HABS) photographs a few years ago. Examining a black-and-white photograph by Ray Moody made on January 21, 1958, I thought about how great it would be to find this house out on the landscape. A short time afterward, I was reading Carroll Van West's *Tennessee's Historic Landscapes: A Traveler's Guide*, and on page 135, there it was. West had provided a recent black-and-white photo and additional information about the place. On January 28, 2005, armed with nothing more than the information that the house was located south of Chuckey in Greene County, I traveled north on TN 351, and crossing the Nicholas P. Earnest Bridge spanning the Nolichuckey River, I looked to my left and saw this most amazing yet representative log house, the very one built around 1784 by Heinrich Ernst.

THE NASHVILLE BASIN'S "CUMBERLAND SETTLEMENTS": MIDDLE TENNESSEE IN 1780

The next most significant settlement hearth for Tennessee formed in Middle Tennessee in the Nashville Basin around 1780. The Cumberland Settlements here were named for the Cumberland River and not for the Cumberland Plateau. Initial settlement began at a point first called French Lick and then Fort Nashborough, a place that eventually became the city of Nashville. From this point, settlements

The Heinrich Ernst (c. 1784) house represents one of the oldest German-built log structures in Tennessee. Also called the Mauris-Earnest Fort house, it was built with V-notched oak logs and is located near Chuckey in Greene County.

rapidly expanded to the immediate east and south of the Cumberland River in the basin. Settlers arrived from two different directions and via two different modes of transportation. The first settlers, explorers really, reached the Nashville vicinity from the Watauga hearth via the Cumberland Gap and overland through central and southern Kentucky, thus approaching the area from the north. James Robertson and other family members led a small party in this way to the area in the fall and early winter of 1779. In due course, other settler groups followed this same overland route by way of Kentucky (Bergeron, Ash, and Keith 1999, 29–39).

Shortly after Robertson's groundbreaking land journey, a second wave of settlers arrived in a flotilla of flatboats, canoes, and other watercraft via the Holston, Tennessee, and Cumberland rivers. Led by John Donelson, the first adventurous group of about 200 people began their journey on December 22, 1779, from the banks of the Holston River at Fort Patrick Henry in the vicinity of Kingsport. Donelson's lead flatboat, appropriately named *The Adventurer*, was a heavy-timbered craft steered by a long sweeping oar at the stern and guided by oarsmen on the sides. A large flatboat carried heavy supplies, perhaps 10 to 20 people, a roof shelter, and even a cooking hearthstone. Flatboats required sufficient shallow draft and adequate river flow to make any reasonable progress downstream. The crudely built vessels were expected to make a one-way journey and then be dismantled at the destination point (Bergeron, Ash, and Keith 1999, 29–33, 37).

The Donelson Party flotilla met with immediate problems on that winter trip because of an unusually low river flow at the time. In two long, cold months, they had inched along only three miles downstream. On February 27, 1780, water levels rose and the group of stalwart individuals—now numbering about 180 men, women, and children, both free and enslaved—pushed off again to continue their journey at a much faster pace, reaching the vicinity of present-day Chattanooga by March 7. Troubles plagued the group: Indian attacks, frostbite, infections, and, most disturbing of all, an outbreak of smallpox. Twenty-eight infected people were quarantined on a single flatboat. As Cherokees pursued the boats at Moccasin Bend, the "sick boat" fell behind and was overtaken by the Indians. All aboard were assumed to have perished. It is speculated that some of the attackers may have contracted smallpox as a result. The rest of the flotilla continued downstream. Another turn of events took place in "the Suck," a whirlpool in the Tennessee River that formed as it passed through the Narrows, a steep, narrow gorge in the Cumberland Plateau. At this point, the boats were spun around in circles until the passengers were ejected one by one downstream.

By March 11, 1780, the flotilla had reached northern Alabama in the vicinity of Muscle Shoals, a wide area of rapids on the Tennessee River. Here the group had expected to find a sign, perhaps a blazed trail that James Robertson was to

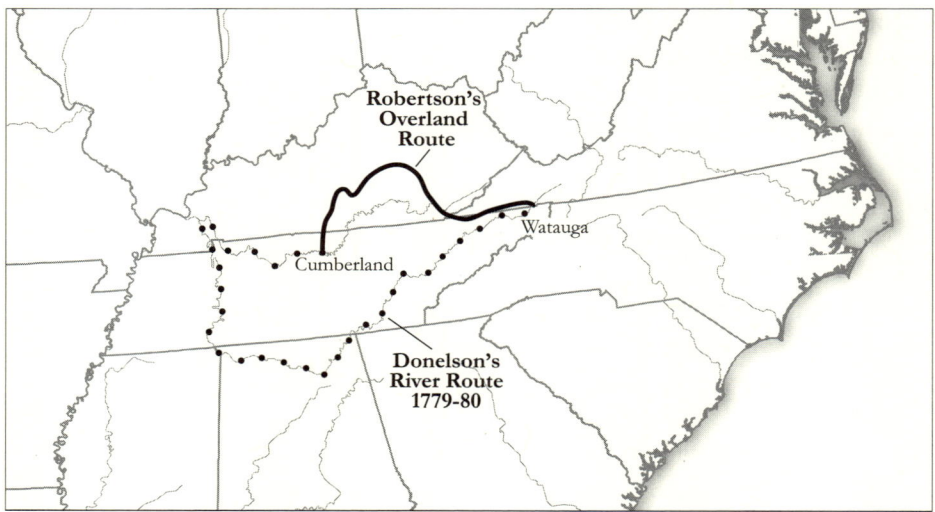

Routes of the Robertson and Donelson parties, which led to settlements in Middle Tennessee in 1780.

have made there to lead them overland northward to the Nashville area. Finding no blaze, the Donelson Party continued rapidly down the Tennessee River and reached the mouth of the Cumberland River on March 24. This last leg of the journey required another hard month of poling and pushing upstream on the Cumberland, which finally took the flotilla to what is now the Nashville area. The Donelson Party lost 33 souls along that cold, dangerous, and daring journey to begin settling Middle Tennessee (Davidson [1946] 1978, 149–66).

FURTHER SETTLEMENT

From the 1780s to about 1840, Tennessee evolved into a more broadly settled region with more settlers emerging and migrating from the two now-ancient hearths: the Watauga Settlements (including North Holston, Carter's Valley, Nolichucky, and especially Watauga) in the northeast and the Cumberland Settlements in the Nashville Basin. By 1800, settlement had expanded southward from the Watauga hearth. Counties in and around Watauga with continuous settlement would later become the present-day Johnson, Sullivan, Hawkins, Hancock, Carter, Unicoi, Washington, Greene, Hamblen, Grainger, Union, Cocke, Jefferson, Knox, Sevier, Blount, and Loudon counties. Physically, the settled area was then bounded by the Cumberland Plateau to the west, the Great Smoky Mountains of the Blue Ridge Province to the east, and the Little Tennessee River to the south.

Surrounding the Nashville vicinity, a large region designated as the North Carolina Military Reservation was established in 1783. The reservation was made up of substantial land grants of 640 acres each, which were awarded to North Carolinian Revolutionary War veterans. Only a few veterans actually accepted grants for direct settlement because of the reservation's great distance from North Carolina and because some veterans simply did not wish to leave their North Carolina homes. However, land-grant parcels could be sold, so land-speculation deals were made with and on behalf of the North Carolina veterans (Bergeron, Ash, and Keith 1999, 34–39). By about 1800, European settlers were moving steadily into the present-day counties of Sumner, Davidson, Robertson, Montgomery, Wilson, Williamson, Smith, and others.

West Tennessee's lands became settled in two large tracts of vacant lands that had become part of a public lands controversy. The Congressional Reservation was established on April 18, 1806, in southwest Middle Tennessee, east of the Tennessee River's western leg. Among the counties settled there between 1807 and 1819 were Maury, Giles, Hickman, Lewis, Lawrence, Perry, and Wayne. The Western Purchase was an enormous region that contained all lands between the western leg of the Tennessee River and the Mississippi River; it was established on October 19, 1818, after the Chickasaw Indians ceded the territory in a treaty (Goodspeed [1887]; Bergeron, Ash, and Keith 1999, 74–76).

Because the lands in the Chattanooga vicinity and surrounding countryside were still held by Cherokees, it would not be until the late 1830s that southeastern Tennessee was settled by Europeans. It would take the atrocities of the "Trail of Tears" in 1837–38—that is, the Cherokee removal from southeastern Tennessee and other areas to what is now Oklahoma—before these lands were open for settlers of European descent (Rehder 2004, 63,71).

To summarize: the two hearths, Watauga (1769) in Upper East Tennessee and the Cumberland Settlements (1780) that formed in Middle Tennessee near Nashville, became the nuclei for future historic folk settlement in Tennessee. Nineteenth-century settlement spread from these two hearths to western and southeastern districts in the state in 1818 and 1838, respectively.

In the next two chapters, we will examine log-construction techniques, types of log folk houses, and log barns and outbuildings on the contemporary Tennessee landscape.

Chapter 3

Log Houses

THE LOG CABIN: SYMBOL, MYTH, OR REALITY?

Now that we have acknowledged Tennessee's early settlement history, we can examine the cultural landscape in which the log cabin symbolizes pioneer spirit as well as shelter. A log cabin may be the definitive representation of frontier life, of a family's struggles with an inhospitable wilderness. The one-room, dirt-floor cabin commands our attention as a sign of poverty before commercial logging and coal mining entered Tennessee.

While the small, ramshackle mountain cabin conveys the most obvious symbolic image of folk housing in Southern Appalachia, there are in fact eight or more meaningful folk-house types on the landscape. Most of these types follow patterns derived from the "pen" tradition, a British way of expressing house units. The term *pen* refers to a room unit with dimensions of approximately 16 feet by 16 feet. To distinguish pen (house) units from crib (barn) units, I tell my students that "pens are for people and cribs are for critters." Houses of the pen tradition include the single-pen type; double-pen houses (two rooms) in subtypes called Cumberland, saddlebag, and dogtrot; larger houses called I-houses (two stories tall, two rooms wide, and one room deep); and four-pen houses (four rooms over four rooms). We also have some twentieth-century floor plans in bungalows and box houses in the region's folk-house typology. I will discuss each of these in detail later in this chapter. (Map 1 in the appendix shows the distribution patterns for all log houses inventoried in the 42-county THC survey.)

Early observers described Tennessee's log dwellings in fascinating ways. In 1853, J. G. M. Ramsey wrote this about a typical log house:

> The dwelling-house, on every frontier in Tennessee, was the log-cabin. A carpenter and mason were not needed to build them—much less the painter, the glazier or the upholsterer. Every settler had, besides his rifle, no other instrument but an axe, a hatchet and a butcher knife. A saw, an augur, a froe and a broad-axe, would supply a whole settlement, and were used as common property in the erection of the log-cabin. The floor of the cabin was sometimes the earth. No saw-mill was yet erected, and, if the means or leisure of the occupant authorized it, he split out puncheons for the floor and for the shutter of the entrance to his cabin. The door was hung with wooden hinges and fastened by a wooden latch.
>
> Such was the habitation of the pioneer Tennesseean. Scarcely can one of these structures, venerable for their years and the associations which cluster around them, be now seen in Tennessee. Time and improvement have displaced them. Here and there, in the older counties, may yet be seen the old log house, which sixty years ago sheltered the first emigrant, or gave, for the time, protection to a neighbourhood, assembled within its strong and bullet-proof walls. (Ramsey [1853], 715–16)

Ramsey's descriptions are remarkable; however, there surely had to have been more log places on the landscape in the early 1850s than Ramsey cared to admit. Perhaps he, like many others, thought of the log house as a crude embarrassment, the antithesis of progress. In the early twentieth century, Horace Kephart said that of 42 houses in the Hazel Creek area on the North Carolina side of the present-day Great Smoky Mountains National Park, "two or three, only, were weather boarded frame houses and attained the dignity of a story and a half" (Kephart [1913], 30–31). The 40 other homes there were log structures. It seems that the dignity of housing became a social issue, with log structures identified as low-quality buildings. Most commonly described was the single-pen cabin, the elemental house type in the region. Other writers of the time observed two-pen houses of the dogtrot, saddlebag, and Cumberland types, and on rare occasions they saw larger two-story dwellings known as I-houses (Rehder 2004, 76–77).

ORIGINS OF AMERICAN LOG BUILDINGS

For much of the eighteenth and nineteenth centuries, log construction was the fundamental building method in Southern Appalachia in general and in much of East and Middle Tennessee in particular. The walls of houses and outbuildings were built of horizontal, rounded, or square-hewn timbers notched at the corners. The typology of corner notches included saddle notch, saddle-V notch, V notch, half-dovetail notch, full-dovetail notch, diamond notch, square notch, semilunate-crown notch, and double notch (Rehder 2004, 86–92; Kniffen 1969, 1–8; Kniffen and Glassie 1966, 40–66). Logs left in the round, but not hewn or squared, used saddle and saddle-V notches. Half logs, split lengthways but left in the round, had semilunate-crown notches. Logs hewn into squared timbers could be notched with the other types, such as half-dovetail, full-dovetail, V, square, and diamond notches.

Who were the first people to build structures with corner-notched horizontal logs in North America? Various culture groups can be eliminated. We can be certain that the Native Americans did *not* originate the technique because their wooden shelters were built with vertical posts and woven saplings. However, within a few years after European contact in the 1750s, some acculturated Cherokees began to adopt crude constructions for rectangular summerhouses using horizontal logs (Cooper 1994, 273–74).

A misconception is that immigrants from the British Isles may have introduced log construction, but the techniques did not exist in Britain at the time of emigration. In fact, none of the immigrant groups from the British Isles had a history or knowledge of using wood in this way (Evans 1974, 53–64; Brunskill 1978, 201). In Northern Ireland's Ulster Province in 1611, Scots were busy erecting structures of stone and thatch just as they had assembled them in Scotland. The English at the same time in the homeland were squaring timbers for half-timbering construction, fastening them with mortise-and-tenon methods, and filling the interstices (the wide spaces between timbers) with stone, brick, and plaster (Carew 1603–24, quoted in Hanna [1902], 1:519–31; Naismith 1985, 20, 24).

The Scotch-Irish had no log-construction technology until they became expert adopters of this method after their arrival in America. The primitive shelters that Scotch-Irish settlers built in 1732 at Kingstree, South Carolina, north of Charleston, were crude excavated earth pits roofed with pine saplings and sand (Witherspoon 1743, cited in Hanna [1902], 2:25–27; Rehder 2004, 80).

Between 1605 and 1720, English settlers in the Chesapeake area were using two construction technologies: *slight framing,* which consisted of vertical posts with small lightweight pieces of wood attached and the whole wall covered in clay, and *box framing*, which employed somewhat more substantial timber-framing methods (Graham, Hudgins, Lounsbury, et al. 2007, 451–66). Neither technology included log construction. Ultimately, the English in New England and the coastal Tidewater region between Virginia and Georgia became well known for building substantial wooden homes with half-timbering construction using timber-frame methods, sawn timbers, mortise-and-tenon joinery, and clapboard siding (Glassie 1975, 124–25; Morrison 1952, 135–39; Rehder 2004, 80–81). Such construction methods were used on Gov. William Blount's mansion, a hall-and-parlor place that dates from 1792 and still stands in Knoxville, Tennessee. It is said that Blount's wife insisted on a proper English-built home even though the sawn lumber had to be transported hundreds of miles overland from the Tidewater region (Mielnik 1998, 74; West 1995, 23, 70–71).

This is not to say that the Chesapeake region was absent of log buildings entirely. Evidence from William Byrd's *History of the Dividing Line* suggests that there were log structures along the North Carolina–Virginia border in 1728 (Byrd [1728] 1967, 94). Also, in some of the old counties in southern Maryland, tax records indicate the presence of log outbuildings in 1798 (Lounsbury 2010, 77–82). But the knowledge of log construction had come there from much earlier sources—from Swedes and Finns in southeastern Pennsylvania. In general, initial settlers from the British Isles did not build log houses because they lacked traditional working knowledge or experience in this type of construction or, as in William Blount's case, they chose not to build or live in such structures because they considered them "improper."

American log construction comes from two European cultural sources: Scandinavians (Swedes and Finns) and Germans. But who brought it here first? Scholars have debated this question for decades. Geographers Terry G. Jordan and Matti Kaups tell us that those responsible for first introducing log construction to America were the Swedes and a few Finns who settled the Delaware River Valley around Philadelphia in 1638–75. Their 1989 book *The American Backwoods Frontier* contains positive evidence for this initial Scandinavian introduction (36–37; 53–63; 79–82). The argument for a German origin comes from Fred Kniffen and Henry Glassie, with support from others (Kniffen and Glassie 1966, 59; Glassie 1978, 538–39; Bucher 1962, 14; Wertenbaker 1938, 298–303). This argument is based on significant log-building cultures with huge immigrant-population diffusions from German-speaking Europe. These immigrants, rich in the traditions of log buildings and corner notching, surely had an important influence on the folk architecture in southeastern Pennsylvania and elsewhere in the Appalachian region (Rehder 2004, 80–81).

May I suggest a compromise between the competing views of log-building origins? I believe that seventeenth-century (1638–75) Swedish and Finnish settlers in the lower Delaware River Valley brought log construction *first* to America.

However, German settlers in the 1710–70 period were responsible for reintroducing, reinforcing, and maintaining log construction in the southeastern Pennsylvania hearth and propelling it to points west and south. Germans and perhaps others actively educated more mobile populations, such as Scotch-Irish immigrants, so that the methods of log construction and notching types that are so closely identified with Appalachia were spread from southeastern Pennsylvania to Tennessee and ultimately through the Upland South, the Ozarks, and westward to central Texas.

In other words, within the Pennsylvania hearth, cultural linkages formed between German users of notching types and Scotch-Irish recipients. As groups of Germans, Scotch-Irish, and other folk progressively migrated down the Great Valley in the Ridge and Valley Province of Southern Appalachia, a process of cultural exchange occurred. I like to think that the Germans were good teachers and that the Scotch-Irish immigrants were good learners (Rehder 2004, 79–81).

CORNER NOTCHING

For four decades, I have researched Tennessee's log buildings in the field. Between 1998 and 2005, I compiled historical buildings survey data from the Tennessee Historical Commission for 42 Tennessee counties distributed across the state. Of the 4,208 log structures for which I analyzed the data, 2,589 were log houses and 1,619 were barns and outbuildings. However, I discovered notch types for only 2,956 structures because many of the buildings were either covered with weatherboarding or the corner notches were not clearly visible. In the pages ahead, I will examine notch types ranging from simple to complex. While this might seem like a straightforward evolution, it is important to note that one notch type did not simply supersede another as building practices became more sophisticated over time. For example, the saddle notch was an old but inefficient simple notch that returned in a renaissance of log housing construction during the Great Depression era.

SADDLE NOTCH

The saddle notch (Map 2) appears with simple rounded cuts made on a round log so that adjacent logs will overlap. Notched cuts can either be on the top or bottom of the log, but the knowledgeable builder only notches the bottom side to prevent rainwater from collecting and thus creating a weak point that will allow the wood to rot. Most beginners needing shelter in a pine forest would use a saddle notch to secure small round pine logs for walls. In 1941, my wife's father built his first house, a two-pen place out of pine logs with saddle notches. "I didn't

The saddle notch, the simplest of notch types, is made on round logs, usually from pine trees.

know any other way to make it," he explained. "I just did what came naturally" (Rehder 2004, 86). Saddle notches are exclusively found on round logs, frequently on round pine logs or on logs from small yellow poplar trees.

In the 42 Tennessee counties that I examined, the saddle notch was represented in 37 counties for at least 1 and up to 85 occurrences. Out of 2,956 structures with notch data, I found 482 saddle-notch occurrences, accounting for 16.3 percent of all notch types. Hawkins County led the way with 85 occurrences (17.6 percent). Other counties with impressive numbers are Johnson, with 40 occurrences (8.2 percent); Knox, with 39 (8 percent); Giles, with 36 (7.4 percent); Davidson, with 33 (6.8 percent); Jackson and Sevier, with 26 (5.3 percent) each; Blount, with 22 (4.5 percent); and Lincoln with 20 (4.1 percent).

By region, East Tennessee counties have 280 (58 percent) of the total 482 saddle-notch occurrences, Middle Tennessee counties have 171 (35.4 percent), and West Tennessee counties have 31 (6.4 percent). We might expect East Tennessee to have more of the total because more counties were surveyed there. However, West and Middle Tennessee are well represented and together account for 202 or

41.9 percent of the 482 saddle notches in the survey. West Tennessee will always have low numbers on any of the log data because fewer counties were surveyed there, not many log structures were ever built in the region, and few have survived. Viewed as a "poor man's" notch, the easy-to-make saddle notch is commonly found on structures throughout the range of rural settlement in the state. However, saddle notches appear most frequently on outbuildings constructed after 1880 and on some houses built between 1930 and 1950 (Rehder 2004, 86).

SADDLE-V NOTCH

The saddle-V notch (Map 3) is a variant combination of a saddle notch and the V notch, an older type with an inverted V-shaped top. Viewed from end on, the saddle-V is pear shaped and appears exclusively on round logs. The top retains the inverted V shape while the bottom of the log remains rounded. The older V notch on hewn squared logs and the saddle-V notch on round ones have the same European origins. However, the saddle-V notches often found in the South on pine and small round poplar timbers are more recent in age and frequently display a lesser quality of workmanship.

Saddle-V notches have a characteristic "V" cut on top of logs that are left in the round.

Log Houses

Is the saddle-V a V notch or a saddle notch? Since it shares its Scandinavian origins with the V notch on hewn logs, the saddle-V notch is, technically speaking, a subtype of the V notch. However, in the South, the saddle-V is more closely identified with saddle notches and as such can be found on outbuildings constructed after 1880, with a greater association with pine log buildings built between 1900 and 1950. There were 162 saddle-V notches in my 42-county survey. They account for a mere 5.4 percent of the 2,956 buildings with notch data. As the map shows, the two counties with the largest numbers of saddle-V notches are Hawkins and Union with 21 (12.9 percent) each. Other representative counties are Johnson with 15 (9.2 percent), Lincoln with 13 (8 percent), and Jackson with 11 (6.7 percent).

V NOTCH

The V notch (Map 4) on hewn squared logs has strong European, especially German and Scandinavian, connections. I am placing it here in the sequence to show how the saddle notch, the saddle-V, and the V notch are related. The V notch is so named because of the inverted V at the top of the log at the butt end. From an end-on perspective, a V-notched log gives the appearance of the gable end of a small house. The V notch in Southern Appalachia is an old notch type when found on large hewn oak or large yellow poplar logs. Frequently, V notches associated with oak timbers are found.

In the survey data of Tennessee counties, the V notch has representation in 29 counties with at least 1 and up to 31 occurrences. The sample survey included 211 buildings with V notches, which accounts for 7.1 percent of all notch types. Tennessee counties with the most notches of the type are Hawkins, with 31 occurrences (14.6 percent), and Johnson, with 21 (9.9 percent). Other nearby counties include Union, with 20 occurrences (9.4 percent), and Hamblen and Washington, with 16 (7.5 percent) each. On the map, notice the heavy concentration of V notches in northeastern Tennessee. Regionally, the V type appears more frequently in the northern half of Appalachia, especially in Pennsylvania, along the Ohio River, and in western Virginia, than it does in the southern half of Appalachia and Tennessee (Rehder 2004, 86–92; Kniffen and Glassie 1966, figure 28).

HALF-DOVETAIL NOTCH

The half-dovetail notch (Map 5) is the most common notch in the southern half of Southern Appalachia and especially in Tennessee. Found on all types of log structures, the half-dovetail is more commonly used on houses, substantial

The V notch is an old notch type made on hewn squared logs.

barns, and small outbuildings where yellow poplar and oak timbers are used. The half-dovetail is an exceptionally good but simple locking notch that sheds water well. From an end view, the half-dovetail displays a sloped cut with a 30–45-degree angle on the upper side. The two vertical sides of the log are straight as is the lower horizontal part of the log. The upper diagonal is the diagnostic trait of the notch.

The half-dovetail notch has exceptional representation. Out of 2,956 structures with notch data, the Tennessee survey revealed an extraordinary total of 1,785 log buildings with half-dovetail notches, accounting for 60.3 percent of

The half-dovetail notch, the most common type in Tennessee, has a characteristic angled cut on top, but the sides are straight and the bottom is horizontal.

all notch types. The range was at least one in every county, and these counties had the highest numbers: Sevier County, with 245 occurrences (13.7 percent); Hawkins, with 205 (11.4 percent); and Giles, with 118 (6.6 percent). In some counties, half-dovetail notches accounted for as much as 68 to 78 percent of the notches there. The map pattern shows two general concentrations: a dominant region in the upper half of East Tennessee from Blount County to the Virginia state line and a second concentration in the southern part of Middle Tennessee's Nashville Basin and southern Highland Rim area of Giles, Lincoln, and adjacent counties.

The half-dovetail notch became a favorite in many parts of Appalachia but particularly in areas beyond the heavily German-settled northern portions of the region. The notch was quite popular in the Upland South and particularly in the southern parts of Southern Appalachia, an area believed to have been settled by larger numbers of Scotch-Irish. We must remember that early settlers from the British Isles apparently knew nothing about how to build with horizontal logs and how to fasten them with corner notches. As I argued earlier, while we should give credit to the early Swedes and Finns in the Delaware River Valley for introducing corner notching to the American landscape, it was the Germans in the culture hearth of southeastern Pennsylvania who taught Scotch-Irish and other immigrant folk the skills they needed to hew logs and to lock them down with corner notches. As settlement expanded, the half-dovetail became the favorite notch, one with deep historical connections to the southeastern Pennsylvania hearth and with European traces in Scandinavia and German-speaking Europe. Thus an association emerged between areas of dominant frequency in half-dovetail notching in the southern half of Southern Appalachia and Tennessee and the dominant log-building cultures of Scotch-Irish and German folk who embraced the region. I see it as a good example of acculturation in folk architecture, where two or more groups exchanged culture traits but with each retaining its own identity (Rehder 2004, 16, 89).

FULL-DOVETAIL NOTCH

A relatively rare notch in America and in Appalachia in particular is the full-dovetail notch (Map 6). There are only 46 occurrences out of 2,956 in the Tennessee analysis—a mere 1.6 percent. The notch is not easy to cut; in fact, I believe it to be the one most difficult to make. From end on, we see that the full-dovetail notch has a 30–45-degree sloped angle on top and another 30–45-degree sloped angle cut on the lower portion of the log but pointing down. When trying to match both slopes to an adjacent log above or below it, the builder finds that the cuts must be precise and the fit exact. The map distribution pattern for full-dovetail notches generally follows the one for half-dovetail notches but with far fewer numbers. In 42 counties of survey data with 46 full-dovetail occurrences, the dominant counties are Hawkins, with 13 (28.2 percent); Giles, with 7 (15.2 percent); Knox, with 5 (10.5 percent); and Sevier, with 4 (8.6 percent). Washington, Blount, and Hardeman counties have 2 occurrences (4.3 percent) each.

DIAMOND NOTCH

Other notch types represented in Tennessee, but in fewer numbers, include the diamond notch, square notch, semilunate-crown, and double notch. One of the

Full-dovetail notches have angled cuts on both the top and bottom while sides remain straight.

rarest notches in America is the diamond notch—as rare as real diamonds, one could say. The diamond notch (Map 7) looks like the diamond symbol on a playing card. The geographic distribution is mostly limited to both sides of the fall line in Virginia and North Carolina, and the notch is largely found on tobacco barns and other small outbuildings there. The 42-county Tennessee survey reveals only 6 out of 2,956 structures. These include 2 structures in Washington County, 1 house illustrated here but destroyed in 1978 in Grainger County, 1 single-crib barn in Marion County, and 1 building each in Hawkins and Cannon counties. These are hardly worth percentage calculation, and the sparse map distribution pattern focuses in northeastern Tennessee. Other diamond-notched

The diamond notch type is as rare as real diamonds. This Grainger County house was razed in 1978.

buildings, however, have been discovered in Middle Tennessee. Michael Gavin, a historic preservationist, cites 2 examples in Davidson County and 1 each in Sumner, Dickson, and Maury counties (Gavin 1997, 15).

SQUARE NOTCH

Square notches (Map 8) are perfectly square as seen from the butt end. The square notch is the weakest connector of the notch types, and buildings using square notches are easily subject to collapse. Oddly, considerable labor is required to

Log Houses

hew and square the logs, yet the square notch cannot lock logs in place, making it a poor alternative indeed. In the survey, I found a surprising 210 structures with square notches in 34 counties. They range from 1 to 24 occurrences and as a group represent 7.1 percent of the 2,956 buildings surveyed. In the counties with square-notched buildings, Sevier County had 24 (11.4 percent), Blount had 23 (10.9 percent), Giles had 23 (10.9 percent), Hawkins had 18 (8.5 percent), and Hardeman had 14 (6.6 percent). For once we find Hawkins County not leading the count. Some buildings are square notched entirely and others have mixed notches of squares, half-dovetails, and others. In later years, as craftsmanship in notching declined, builders may have become less precise and accidentally produced a square notch when their goal was to make a half-dovetail (Rehder 2004, 90).

It is not unusual to find different notch types in the same building, as on this structure in Hancock County.

SEMILUNATE-CROWN NOTCH

The semilunate-crown notch is formed on half logs. A builder takes round logs, splits them in half lengthways, cuts small curved notches in the bottom of each, and assembles them in much the same way as he would a saddle notch. The semilunate-crown, named because it appears as a half moon, is rare in Tennessee. I did not map these, but I found a total of 12 occurrences in my 42-county data: 4 (33.3 percent) in Grainger County, 4 (33.3 percent) in Hawkins, 2 (16.6 percent) in Blount, 1 (8.3 percent) in Johnson, and 1 (8.3 percent) in Hardeman. None of these structures appear to be especially old and are likely a twentieth-century phenomenon.

DOUBLE NOTCH

The double notch (Map 9) is quite rare on the American landscape, though popularized by the "Lincoln Logs" children's toy. I found 32 occurrences in the Tennessee data, and some are on late-model log buildings in and around state park recreational areas built in the 1930s. These were camp structures built while the parks were being established and appear in only five of the counties surveyed. Davidson County, a quite urban county with Nashville as its center, dominates with 25 (78.1 percent) double-notched homes that appear to have been built in the 1930s but may date from the1920s–40s period. These places are probably not folk houses but rather were built from architectural plans in urban and state park locales. Elsewhere, especially in Scandinavia, double-notched log buildings are common folk structures (Kniffen 1969; Kniffen and Glassie 1966; Jordan and Kaups 1989, 135–62; Jordan 1985, 55, 57, 91–93).

REGIONAL PATTERNS OF NOTCH TYPES

We are fortunate that all of the notch types discussed above are represented in Tennessee, but they display variable patterns in their larger regional geographic distribution. Looking beyond Tennessee for a moment to the eastern United States, we find saddle notches with a broad sweep of dominance in the Lowland South, south and east of the fall line along the inner coastal plain of the Carolinas and Georgia and clearly dominating the inner Gulf Coastal Plain of Alabama, Mississippi, non-French interior Louisiana, and going well into Arkansas and Texas. Saddle notches and pine trees correlate well because saddle notches are always cut on round logs and most pine trees remain slender with small diameters. So, not surprisingly, the geographic distribution for the saddle notch corresponds exactly to the distribution of the southern pine forests.

North of Tennessee, the V notch finds its largest geographic distribution beginning in its hearth in Pennsylvania and clearly dominating in a broad westward sweep of the Ohio River Valley through southern Ohio, Indiana, Illinois, and out across Missouri. The less common saddle-V notch is used with round pine and poplar logs and shows some affinity with the northern pattern of V notches. However, the saddle-V does not follow the exact geographic distribution as the saddle notch. But in Tennessee, the saddle and saddle-V share a common general distribution and a time frame for construction from about 1900 to about 1940. The diamond notch, though rare in all parts of the eastern United States, has a concentration along either side of the fall line in the Virginia and North Carolina Piedmont. Its distribution does not cover a broad area, but its rare appearance forms a quasi-boundary to the east of Appalachia (Kniffen and Glassie 1966, figure 28; Rehder 2004, 91–92).

Which notch is most common in the region? Clearly, the half-dovetail notch dominates the southern half of Southern Appalachia south of the New River in the Great Valley of Virginia, and in my analysis of the data on Tennessee's log buildings it reigns supreme, with over 60 percent of all buildings surveyed. As for the northern half of Southern Appalachia, northeast from the New River, especially beyond Roanoke, the V notch dominates but is closely followed by half-dovetail notches and, in Pennsylvania, even full-dovetails (Rehder 2004, 92).

TIMBER TYPES

Forest species of timbers used in historic log constructions can tell us about the forest ecology of Tennessee. I have prepared distribution maps of the data from fieldwork and from the Tennessee Historical Commission's surveys of 42 counties. I am not as confident as I would like to be with these data because I mostly worked with archival photographs and often did not make direct field observations for many of the sites. The maps show timber patterns per county for yellow poplar, oak, pine, and cedar. Other timber species, not mapped here, were certainly present because settlers logically selected appropriate trees in close proximity to house sites.

Yellow poplar trees (Map 10) were clearly the trees of choice in the initial occupance and early settlement periods (1769–1870). I share a common belief that of all timber types, yellow poplar is absolutely superior for the construction of log buildings. The mature tree has a tall, straight trunk with only a few limbs in the uppermost part. The logs are lightweight and easily moved. The wood is soft and thus easy to cut and hew, resistant to insects and rot, and incredibly durable. A folk-house builder benefited tremendously when he could use yellow poplars.

The Cherokee name for yellow poplar trees was *tsiyu*, which translates as "canoe"; this alone offers sufficient evidence for the aboriginal use of the tree (King, Blankenship, and Duncan 2006, 31, 75). While the Cherokees used yellow poplar for dugout canoes, they did not construct log buildings until after European settlers arrived. The best concentration of yellow poplar timbers can be found in the East Tennessee counties of Johnson, Hawkins, Grainger, Union, Sevier, and Blount. A second region centers on Giles, Lincoln, and Maury counties in southern Middle Tennessee.

In a second phase of log-building construction, timber types included oak and mixtures of oak, chestnut, poplar, and pine. Thus, a change to the use of some hardwoods is indicated. Also indicated are changes in the availability of timber suitable for log-house construction on specific sites. The map of oak timbers (Map 11) shows a wide distribution, with concentrations in much of East Tennessee, another in the Nashville Basin (especially in Davidson and Giles counties), and a third area on the Eastern Highland Rim that includes Jackson, Overton, Putnam, White, and Warren counties.

With the third phase came the use of softer pine species (Map 12). These are poor choices because they are knotty, resinous, and prone to decay. From the late 1880s to the 1930s, and for years thereafter, softer pine species were about the only sizeable trees remaining on the landscape suitable for log construction. The map pattern of pine species indicates a concentration in Johnson, Hawkins, Union, and Sevier counties in East Tennessee simply because there were so many log structures there in the inventory. However, the broad, statewide map pattern for pine species illustrates the widespread use of available pine trees for log construction. The map of cedar timbers (Map 13) correlates beautifully with limestone soils on limestone geology. The Nashville Basin dominates in cedars for that reason. It is little wonder that just east of Nashville is the Cedars of Lebanon State Park.

To summarize: I have notch data on 2,956 structures. In rank order for the top seven notches, the pattern for occurrences are these: half-dovetail, 1,785; saddle, 482; V notch, 211; square notch, 210; saddle-V, 162; full-dovetail, 46; and double notch, 32. For the diamond and semilunate-crown, the occurrences were 12 or less each. In terms of rarity, the diamond notch lives up to its name with only 6 out of 2,956 notch occurrences. Chosen timber types evolved temporally from yellow poplar to oak to pine, while cedar and other species like chestnut were site specific. The use of horizontal logs with corner notches was a European introduction that came first from Swedish and Finnish sources in the 1600s, then later in the 1700s from German source areas. The primary arrival point in North America for these techniques was southeastern Pennsylvania, from which emerged one of America's unique symbols, the log cabin.

FOLK HOUSE TYPES

House types reflect the personality of a culture and its region by representing the folk who built them. They help us trace the migrations of folk cultures by becoming diagnostic culture traits that sometimes identify culture or ethnic groups. They inspire us to seek answers to questions about place of origin, routes and times of diffusion, floor plans, construction materials, and levels of diagnostic ethnic identity.

The most common folk house types in Tennessee are patterned after the pen tradition in which a pen represents an individual room unit. The typology comprises the following: (1) single-pen; (2) double-pen (two rooms), with subtypes called Cumberland, saddlebag, and dogtrot; (3) the I-house, which is characterized by two-story height, two-room width, and one-room depth; and (4) the four-pen dwelling with four rooms over four rooms. Construction techniques and materials for folk houses may include horizontal, rounded, or square-hewn logs with corner notches, framed sawn lumber, brick, or even stone. But here, of course, we will focus on the log structures.

SINGLE-PEN HOUSES

The single-pen house (Map 14) is the source from which other houses in the pen tradition evolve. A typical one-room cabin measures about 20 feet by 17 feet and has a single outside chimney at the end of one gable. Most houses have a single story, but some are built with a story and a half to include a sleeping loft supported by mortised loft joists in the ceiling above the primary room. A ladder or a stairway leads to the loft, where the family's children could sleep. A single front door, single back door, and optional windows provide access, air, and light to the humble dwelling. Appendages—that is, additional structural attachments not considered in the typology of the single-pen—may include front and rear porches, and a kitchen in the back.

In my analysis of historical buildings survey data in the THC archives, I found that within a total of 4,208 log structures, 2,589 were log houses, and of that there were 970 (37.4 percent) single-pens. The majority of log single-pens are in these physiographic regions: the Blue Ridge, Ridge and Valley, Cumberland Plateau, Eastern Highland Rim, and Nashville Basin. Many counties west of Nashville have not been surveyed, but among those that have, fewer log buildings turned up. The 970 single-pens were the most numerous of all log building types in the survey data, far outnumbering the 433 Cumberland houses, 294 saddlebags, and 287 dogtrots in the double-pen group.

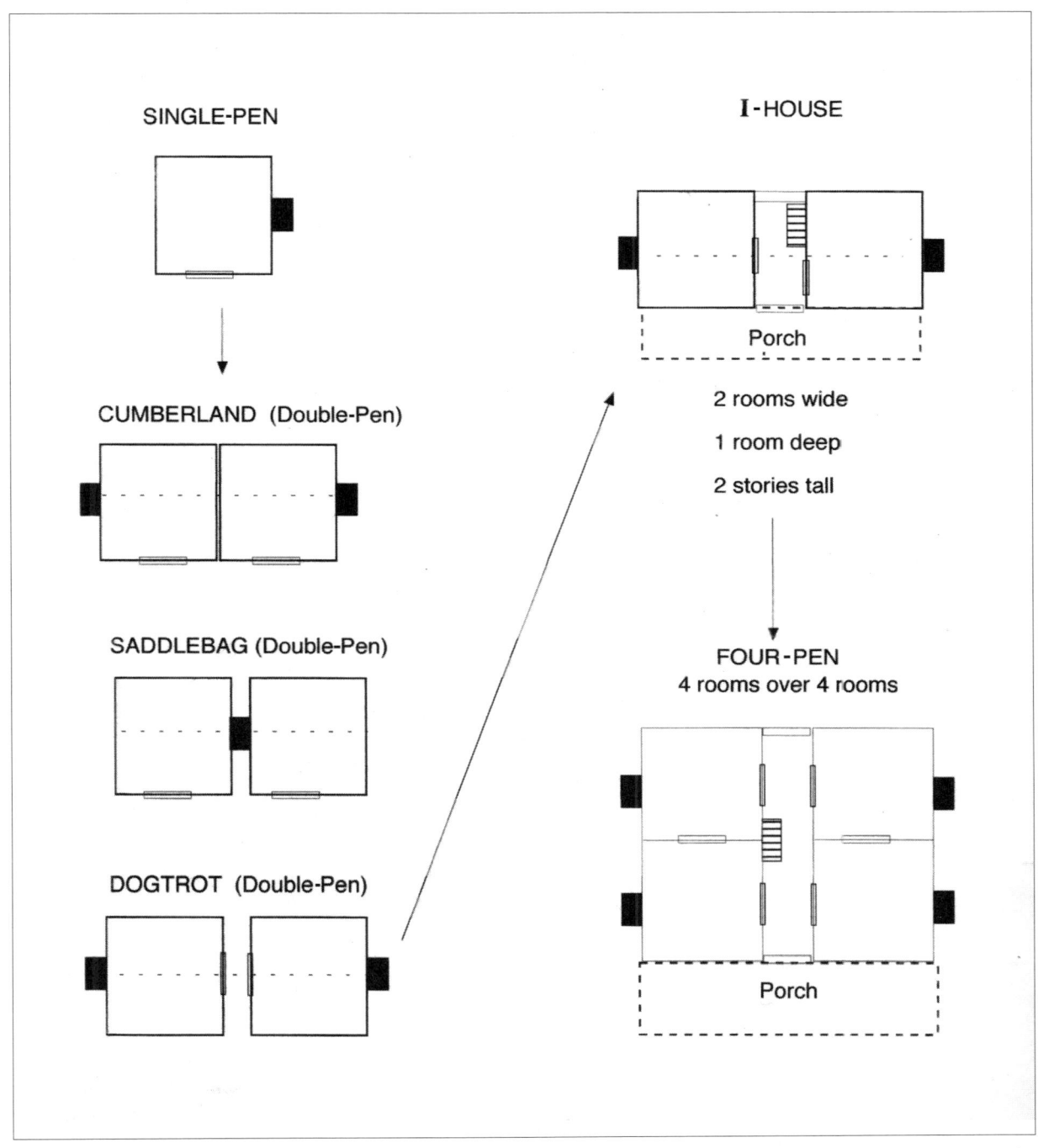

House types evolved from the single-pen to three double-pen types to the I-house and finally to the four-pen with floor plans that follow the British pen tradition. (Sources: Kniffen 1965; Jordan and Kaups 1989; Rehder 2004)

At the county level, single-pens ranged from as few as 4 houses in Chester County in West Tennessee to as many as 121 in Hawkins County in East Tennessee. The top counties were Hawkins, with 121 (12.4 percent); Sevier, with 62 (6.3 percent); Lincoln, with 49 (5 percent); Giles, with 46 (4.7 percent); Dekalb, with 46 (4.7 percent); Overton. with 41 (4.2 percent); Marshall, with 39 (4 percent); Knox. with 37 (3.8 percent); and Blount, Jefferson, and Maury with 36 (3.7 percent) each.

Single-pens are not always square. They may be small rectangles measuring approximately 20–22 feet long by 16–18 feet deep. The dimensions represent an unusual uniformity for dwellings constructed nearly two centuries ago and built by folk builders with no blueprints. One could surmise that the dimensions were governed by tree type and size, or by the weight of the logs. Measurement might have been based on pacing the distance, or by a number of axe handles, or by some other means. Could it have been based on a traditional measurement from Europe? A standardized British measurement was the rod, a 16-foot unit used for measuring land, house bays or room units, and barns. The rod originated as a measure for animal stalls when 16 feet by 16 feet was the space needed for two pair of oxen (Addy 1898, 17, 66–69, cited by Wilson 1971, 9; Addy 1933, 195–215, cited by Houston 1963, 118, and by Rehder 2004, 99). This legendary dimension came to the American colonies as the house bay. The 16-foot bay remained to become the basis for the single-pen, bay, or square cabin of the English pen tradition (Glassie 1978, 543–45; Glassie 1963, 9; Wilson 1971, 9–10; Wilson 1975, 54–55). Henry Glassie's early research on the southern mountain cabin interpreted the square cabin as English and the rectangular cabin of 22 feet by 16 feet as Scotch-Irish. According to Glassie, the rectangular cabin was a direct descendent of dwelling dimensions from western Britain and Northern Ireland (Glassie 1978, 529, 543–53; Rehder 2004, 99).

In Grainger County, John Morgan and Joy Medford, members of my historic structures survey team in 1978, analyzed 54 log single-pens. The houses had average dimensions of 22 feet by 18 feet and were built between 1793 and 1930. Twenty-four of the houses were built before 1860. Thirty-seven of the 54 houses were notched with half-dovetails, and 12 houses were V notched. Three major timber types were represented: 21 houses were built with pine logs, 17 with yellow poplar, 4 with oak, and the remaining houses with mixtures of timber types (Morgan and Medford 1980, 137–58, 152–56).

Inventorying adjacent Union County, Vincent Ambrosia, another member of my survey team, compiled data on 49 log single-pens in 1979. Pen dimensions were similar to those in Grainger County. Forty-two houses, or 85.7 percent, were built with half-dovetail notches. The few remaining notch types were represented by 2 houses with V notches, 3 houses with saddle notches, 1 house with

The single-pen house, the simplest house in the pen tradition, has just one room and usually one chimney. This one in Rhea County near Washington has mortised loft joists above the door and windows to support an interior ceiling/floor for a sleeping loft upstairs.

saddle-V notches, and 1 house with square notches. In terms of timber types, 35 houses were built of yellow poplar timbers, 6 were built of oak, 6 were of pine, and the remainder were mixed (Ambrosia 1979, 10, 14).

John Morgan's research in Blount County in 1982–84 revealed a total of 123 log single-pen houses, of which 70 percent were square and 30 percent were rectangular. Popular dimensions of single-pens were, in feet, 26 by 20, 25 by 20, 26 by 18, 24 by 18, 25 by 17, 24 by 16, 22 by 16, and 20 by 15. Morgan's analysis of all surveyed log house types in Blount County revealed that 24 percent used V notches and 58 percent used the more common half-dovetail notches. Moreover, representative timber types were pine (68 percent), oak (11 percent), and yellow poplar (an astonishingly low 5 percent) (Morgan 1990, 28–29, 34–36). Morgan's 123 inventoried log single-pens largely came from the warmer and lower-elevation Ridge and Valley portions of the county, which is dominated by pine, oak, and, to a much lesser degree, yellow poplar trees. That the Great Smoky Mountains National Park occupies a third or more of the county's area also partially

Log Houses

accounts for the difference. The higher availability of pine habitat outside the park and at lower elevations would account for the higher number of pine structures surviving there.

Let's examine Union and Grainger counties, surveyed in the late 1970s, as examples. The dominant notches on single-pen houses were half-dovetail, with 68.5 percent in Grainger County and 85.7 percent in Union County. The V notch, however, accounted for only 22.2 percent in Grainger County and 1 percent in Union County. Regarding age, the Grainger County study showed that half-dovetail-notched single-pen houses dated from the 1790s to 1915 (Morgan and Medford 1980, 152–56; Reding 2002, 41–51).

Timber types indicated changing availability and wood choices in the 1978–79 surveys for the two counties. In Union County, yellow poplar timbers were used to construct 61.4 percent of log dwellings (Ambrosia 1979, 10). For Grainger County, a three-phase temporal pattern emerged. Initially, yellow poplar timbers dominated 53 percent of log single-pens in the early first phase (1790s–1850). In the middle phase (1850–80), oak and mixtures of oak, poplar, chestnut, and some pine timbers were used. For the last phase (1880–1930), pine timbers dominated in 81 percent of the single-pen houses (Morgan and Medford 1980, 152–56).

Selected Single-pens

About 10 miles north of Rogersville, in Hawkins County at the Eidson Post Office on state highway TN 70, is a single-pen with half-dovetail notches on oak logs. A huge limestone chimney anchors the east side of the structure. The stones in the chimney are smooth dressed, meaning that they were sized and cut by a professional stonemason, perhaps one of the mysterious Italian stonecutters who once made a living traveling about East Tennessee and doing odd stone-masonry jobs. Such work is still evident on old buildings and bridges throughout the area. A shake roof and shake-covered front porch complete the ensemble. The building's dimensions are about 16 feet by 18 feet, it appears to have been a restoration project, and it was perhaps a small museum or antique shop. Cattle now graze in its yard, while just yards away are the current and past (c. 1950s) post offices for the Eidson community.

Up on the Cumberland Plateau in Putnam County off Exit 280 of I-40, Baxter Road goes south and intersects with Mine Lick Creek Road. There lies a log single-pen to which I gave the number PM002 because it was not included in the Tennessee Historical Commission's database. The original structure had been a two-pen house—likely a saddlebag built in stages, with one log pen on the west

Ignored by grazing cattle, this restored single-pen at Eidson in Hawkins County appears to be abandoned.

Not much is known of this single-pen with half-dovetail notches on huge yellow poplar logs. Once weather boarded, it had escaped the historical buildings survey in 1982 in Putnam County. The author stumbled upon it twenty-three years later.

side and a framed (perhaps board-and-batten) pen to the east. The absence of a chimney on the west elevation tells me that the house is neither a Cumberland nor dogtrot type, houses that have gable-end chimneys. The log pen may have been covered earlier with weatherboarding and perhaps went unnoticed as a log structure when surveyors came by in 1983. The framed east pen is now gone, but the west log pen is in good shape as evidenced by the roof, former siding, and condition of the logs. The notches are beautifully hewn half-dovetails on yellow poplar and oak logs. The structure measures approximately 15 feet by 18 feet, and my estimated date for it is between 1850 and 1880.

DOUBLE-PEN HOUSES

As families grew, the need for more space called for additional log pens, sometimes resulting in double-pen houses. This evolutionary process of building in stages, a pen at a time, was about as common as constructing two pens at once. Double-pens come to us in three types: the Cumberland house (once called the basic or standard double-pen), the saddlebag house, and the dogtrot house. Each double-pen house has two room units, or pens, placed side to side, one-room depth, single-story height, and a common saddle roof along the long axis. Chimney placement, number of chimneys, and spacing of pens are the diagnostic traits that distinguish subtypes.

Cumberland House

This house (Map 15) takes its name from the Cumberland Plateau, where in the 1970s University of Tennessee anthropologists Riedl, Ball, and Cavender found it to have remarkable dominance in the TVA's Normandy Reservoir Project area in Coffee County, Tennessee. The late Professor Bert Riedl, an Austrian-born cultural anthropologist and a close friend and colleague of mine, and his research assistants Tony Cavender and Donald Ball coined the name "Cumberland" for this rather ordinary-looking two-pen house. It is quite fitting that I honor Bert Riedl by using the term "Cumberland house" in my teaching and published professional work (Riedl, Ball, and Cavender 1976, cited by Jordan 1985, 24, 28, 146–49; Jordan and Kaups 1989, 209–10; Rehder 2004, 101–2; and Ball 2006).

    A Cumberland house has two pens joined at the center, a chimney at the end of each of the two gables, and at least one but usually two front doors. Windows and appendages of front and back porches and an attached kitchen in back add to the structure. A Cumberland house may be constructed of logs or of framed

The Cumberland house type, a double-pen, has two rooms joined in the middle and end chimneys. It may have one or two front doors on the long axis. This example is found in Middle Tennessee near Murfreesboro.

sawn planks, but like other small folk houses in Southern Appalachia, it is seldom built of brick or stone.

The survey data showed a total of 433 Cumberland houses or 16.7 percent of the 2,589 log houses surveyed. For East Tennessee, there were 27 (6.2 percent) log Cumberland houses in Hawkins County, 15 (3.4 percent) in Johnson County, 13 (3 percent) each in Jefferson and Sevier counties, 12 (2.7 percent) in Blount County, 12 (2.7 percent) in Loudon County, 10 (2.3 percent) in Hamblen County, and 7 (1.6 percent) in Knox County. Farther west, in the Cumberland Plateau region, I found 51 log Cumberland houses in Overton County alone, or 11.7 percent of the total of 433. White County has 11 such houses (2.5 percent), while Grundy County, entirely on the southern part of the Cumberland Plateau, has 9 (2 percent). On the northern rim are Clay County with 15 (3.4 percent) and Macon County with 24 (5.5 percent). I examined only log houses, not framed ones, so there are likely hundreds more on the landscape. Regardless of log or framed construction, Cumberland houses are clearly identified with the plateau and rim subregions in Tennessee in particular and the western parts of the Upland South and Southern Appalachia in general.

In 1992, I wrote that the Cumberland house appeared more frequently in some areas of the South but at later time periods when balloon framing with sawmill lumber had become popular (Rehder 1992, 107–8; Wilson 1975, 78; Rehder 2004, 102). Let us now examine where the Cumberland house fits into the scheme of things over time. In 2004, I reported on a 17-county sample that found 138 houses of the type out of 658 total log homes, or about 21 percent. For the counties on the Cumberland Plateau in the 2004 data, there were 106 occurrences out of the 138 total log Cumberland houses. This yielded an impressive 76.8 percent of the log houses of this type for that specific subregion (Rehder 2004, 102). However, in my current and larger 42-county data set, the log Cumberland house represents 433 of all 2,589-log houses or 16.7 percent. Both total percentages—21 in 2004 and 16.7 more recently—are particularly close. From a broader perspective, Cumberland houses are commonly distributed on the western margins of Appalachia in the Cumberland and Allegheny Plateau regions. The house type also can be traced farther west into the Nashville Basin, to Arkansas, and beyond. Also, it is well documented in Kentucky in the Bluegrass Basin, Pennyroyal, and places farther west.

Saddlebag House

A saddlebag house (Map 16) has a single central chimney with a pen built on each side of it. Like other multipen structures, this double-pen house in its formative stages could be built first as a single-pen; then the second pen would be added at a later time. To understand the origins of the name, imagine the chimney as a "horse" and the pens on each side as "saddlebags" (Kniffen 1965, 561; Carlisle 1982, 46–76; Rehder 2004, 103–4).

A fine example of a log saddlebag house is the Noah "Bud" Ogle place in the Great Smoky Mountains National Park in Sevier County near Gatlinburg. Take US 441 to traffic light number 8 in the center of Gatlinburg. Travel east on Airport Road up the mountain, where the road name becomes Cherokee Orchard Road as you enter the park. The Ogle farm complex with its saddlebag house and four-crib barn is two miles up the road and on the right. The saddlebag's overall dimensions by elevation are 45 feet 3 inches east; 44 feet 9 inches west; 17 feet 10 inches north; and 18 feet 3 inches south. The older north pen is 19 feet 11 inches wide and 17 feet 10 inches deep. The south elevation's pen is 20 feet 2 inches wide and 18 feet 3 inches deep. The chimney measures 4 feet 11 inches wide. Since the house was built in stages, the newer south pen is the larger one. In 1879, Noah "Bud" Ogle and his wife, Cindy, started the 400-acre farm on steep, rocky land that was blessed with trees and streams. In time they added a small, tub mill–

A saddlebag house has a central chimney (the "horse") and a pen on either side (the "saddlebags"). Pictured here are the east and north (gable) elevations of the Noah "Bud" Ogle place in the Great Smoky Mountains National Park (Sevier County).

type gristmill, springhouse, other cribs and enclosures, and built a huge, four-crib log barn. Superbly restored in the 1960s, this log house and existing four-crib barn with original chestnut logs are the best example structures that remain. The reconstructed tub mill operates on a creek site 200 yards west of the saddlebag house. In chapter 5, I discuss another interesting saddlebag called the Hamilton-Tolliver place in Union County northeast of Maynardville.

The analysis of 2,589 log houses in the 42-county Tennessee survey shows 294 log saddlebags, or 11.3 percent of all log houses. The map pattern for the saddlebag type, however, appears to be unusually well represented in sampled counties in East Tennessee's Ridge and Valley Province. There were 34 (11.5 percent) in Hawkins County, 12 (4 percent) in Blount County, 11 (3.7 percent) in Jefferson County, and 7 (2.3 percent) in adjacent Hamblen County. The Union County survey revealed just 7 log saddlebag houses (2.3 percent), all of which were built with half-dovetail notches (Ambrosia 1979, 14).

Saddlebag houses, as shown on the map, are more prevalent on the Cumberland Plateau and Eastern Highland Rim. Jackson County has 33 (11.2 percent) of the saddlebags. White County has 15 (5.1 percent), Sequatchie County has 10

(3.4 percent), and Overton County has 24 (8.1 percent). They also appear in convincing patterns in the adjacent Nashville Basin and Kentucky's Bluegrass Basin and Pennyroyal regions. John Morgan and I once believed that framed, sawnwood saddlebags outnumbered log saddlebags in Appalachia's Ridge and Valley and Blue Ridge Provinces, on landform regions other than the plateau country (Morgan 1986). But if all saddlebag houses—framed, log, or otherwise—were analyzed, there still would be a much wider distribution throughout Southern Appalachia but with special concentrations in the southern Cumberland Plateau and Highland Rim country of Tennessee (Rehder 2004, 103–4).

Dogtrot House

The dogtrot house (Map 17) is perhaps one of the most easily recognized folk houses on the American landscape. This double-pen house has two pens separated by an open passage or breezeway, a feature colloquially called a *dogtrot*,

By 1958, the Noah "Bud" Ogle saddlebag was deteriorating, as evident in this view of the south and west elevations. (Library of Congress, Prints and Photographs Division, Historical American Buildings Survey, HABS TN-122–1. Photo by Jack E. Boucher, Nov. 3, 1958.)

A fascinating house type, the dogtrot features an open breezeway between two pens. This site was near Hohenwald (Lewis County), 12 miles southwest of the Meriwether Lewis National Monument. (Library of Congress, Prints and Photographs Division, Historical American Buildings Survey, HABS TN-36. Photo by A. A. Gustafson, Aug. 1937.)

which comes directly from folk traditions. Fred B. Kniffen, dean of American folk geography, did not make it up. Here we are clearly in the realm where vernacular means vernacular—that is, the point where *folk language* and *folk culture* intersect, a point where scholars can only be observers. We cannot be certain of the term's origins, only that it is well ingrained in the folk cultures where such structures reside. Ask older people in rural Middle or West Tennessee or in the Ozarks about dogtrots, and they likely will know what they are and will know them by that name.

The actual "dogtrot," that open-air breezeway between the two pens, is the dominant diagnostic trait of the house, which is sometimes described as "two pens and a passage" but should always be called a dogtrot house. Outside chimneys match the outside gable ends. Doors to each pen usually appear in the open-air dogtrot, but on some houses they may be on the front. The breezeway may be enclosed on some houses, especially remodeled ones where the owners sought to provide a heated and air-conditioned hall or den. From my own experience, I have found that on hot summer days the cool, refreshing breeze passing through the dogtrot between the pens is most welcome.

My four decades of exploring southern mountain landscapes has turned up an unusual distribution pattern for the dogtrot. I have not seen a log dogtrot north of Virginia. The house is rare east of the Blue Ridge Province, absent east of the Piedmont, and surprisingly rare in East Tennessee. The house has an inconsistent

Log Houses

Dogtrot houses, like this one in Giles County, sometimes have the breezeway enclosed to form a central hallway.

distribution in Kentucky, where it is very weak in eastern Kentucky but has better distribution in central Kentucky in the Bluegrass Basin; one finds it especially in southern Kentucky in the Pennyroyal (Montell and Morse 1976, 21). As my Tennessee map pattern shows, the dogtrot is best represented in Middle Tennessee on the Cumberland Plateau, Highland Rim, and in the Nashville Basin, and out towards West Tennessee. The dogtrot house also spreads westward into Arkansas and the Missouri Ozarks. Dogtrots sweep solidly southward from Middle Tennessee throughout much of Alabama, Mississippi, northern and western Anglo Louisiana, and well into east and central Texas (Rehder 2004, 104–7; Jordan-Bychkov 2003, 36–40; Jordan and Kaups 1989, 179–96; Wilson 1975, 32–43).

On the Southern Appalachian landscape, however, the dogtrot house is almost an abnormality. A close examination of Jordan and Kaups's detailed map of dogtrot house distributions in their book *The American Backwoods Frontier* shows only 4 occurrences of the log dogtrot in Pennsylvania, 4 in Virginia, 2 in West Virginia, and 3 in South Carolina. John Morgan reported a total of 16 log dogtrots in East Tennessee's Grainger, Blount, Morgan, and Union counties (Morgan 1990, 31). I know of additional observed examples to modify Morgan's total. In my 42-county study, 15 counties in East Tennessee's Ridge and Valley region had a total of 21 log dogtrots out of 998 log houses, or 2.1 percent. Sadly, these are extremely meager figures for the East Tennessee subregion. Even Hawkins, the county richest in log structures in Tennessee, had only 4 log dogtrots out of 287 log houses, or 1.3 percent.

On the Cumberland Plateau, one finds many more dogtrots. In my data analysis of log houses, there were 287 log dogtrot houses, or 11 percent of the total 2,589 surveyed. Most of them are on the Cumberland Plateau and Highland Rim with concentrations in a straight-line north-to-south pattern in the plateau counties of Overton, with 12 occurrences (4.1 percent); Putnam, with 4 (1.3 percent); Sequatchie, with 13 (4.5 percent); Grundy, with 5 (1.7 percent); and Marion, with 6 (2 percent).

The Highland Rim counties have many log dogtrots. For example, Dekalb County boasts 33 such houses (11.4 percent), Giles has 24 (8.3 percent), Macon 14 (4.8 percent), and Jackson 11 (3.8 percent). The Nashville Basin displays good representation, with Maury County having 35 log dogtrots (12.1 percent), Marshall County 22 (7.6 percent), and Davidson County 22 (7.6 percent). The log dogtrot house clearly has strength in numbers in the Cumberland Plateau, Highland Rim, and Nashville Basin. Gaining momentum in the Nashville Basin, it expands through the Deep South all the way to Texas. In a very graphic way, the dogtrot seems to follow the Natchez Trace from Nashville to Natchez, Mississippi, a route that funneled settlers and settlement forms towards Texas. The log dogtrot also appears to follow the route of the 1838 "Trail of Tears" of the Cherokee from southeastern Tennessee to eastern Oklahoma (Rehder 2004, 106).

Dogtrot Discoveries: Northeast of Nashville, Clay County hugs the border with Kentucky, and the land along TN 52 that runs westward from the county seat of Celina through Moss and on to Red Boiling Springs in Macon County just seems to roll along without much fuss, neither flat nor steep. However, the land north and south of Celina found along TN 53 has more surface roughness, a bit more steepness, and displays the serrated edges of the Highland Rim country. Some time ago, I was north of Celina, east of the Cumberland River, which enters the region from Kentucky in the north. To my west was Dale Hollow Lake, a man-made reservoir on the Obey River. My GPS was confused that day because a new road had been built there. I turned off highway TN 53 to go to Thompson's Store and from there to search for site CY307, a single-pen house. After much time, effort, and a few rough miles, I reached the poultry farm of Lonnie Daniels—or "Mr. Dan'ils," as he says it—and he told me that the house I sought had been torn down. However, he knew of some other log houses located at nearby Holly Camp on Dale Hollow Lake. He added that one of the log houses was a dogtrot and that his wife's family had once owned it. The new owners, he said, had moved it from its original site in Kentucky to its present site near the lake. After thanking him, I went off to find it, and, yes, he was right: the place was a classic dogtrot, though without the chimneys. The yellow poplar logs were notched with half-dovetail notches. I estimated the size of each pen at 16 by 16 feet with an 8-foot-wide dogtrot passage. I labeled this property CY000. Next door, to the west on the same property, was a single-pen house with mortised loft joists, half-dovetail notches on yellow poplar logs, and no chimney. Perhaps this structure was moved there as well, but Daniels had not indicated its origin. I estimated the size of the house as 16 by 16 feet.

In late January 2005 in White County, I ran across an unusual log dogtrot house at the White County Fairgrounds on the northern edge of Sparta, the county seat. I had been following my GPS to another site, but the road I sought was blocked. So I went onto the fairgrounds and there it was. I knew nothing of the place when I first saw it. Later, while reading the book *Upper Cumberland Historic Architecture* by W. Calvin Dickinson, Michael E. Birdwell, and Homer D. Kemp, I learned more about the mysterious dogtrot, which was called the John White House. John White, a Virginian for whom the county was named, had

White County is named for John White, a Revolutionary War veteran. His dogtrot house was built in 1808 in Hickory Valley just south of Sparta. In the 1990s, it was moved to this site on the White County Fairgrounds just north of Sparta.

served with George Washington at Valley Forge and had received a land grant for his military role in the Revolutionary War. Built in 1808, the house was originally located at the southern end of Hickory Valley near Caney Creek (see the "private investigator" story in chapter 1). Later it was covered with clapboard siding. In the 1990s, the house was moved several miles north to the present White County Fairgrounds location (Dickinson, Birdwell, and Kemp 2002, 20–21). There the building was restored to a more authentic look with exposed logs—the way we see it today. The logs are yellow poplar with V notches. One pen is built as a two-story unit while the other pen is a story and a half in height. This two-level appearance is a bit like the 1960s split-level house where I lived for 32 years in Knoxville. Double-pen houses with such uneven pens or offset heights are rare, but they do appear here and there. For another example of a double-pen with uneven units, see the "house that moved" in chapter 5.

Dogtrot Origins: Surprisingly, the origin of the dogtrot house type is indefinite. Some prominent scholars say it is of Scandinavian origin (Scofield 1936, 229–40; Wright 1958; Jordan 1985, 146, 149; Jordan and Kaups 1989, 179–96, 249). Fred Kniffen locates the first appearance of the dogtrot house in southeastern Tennessee (Kniffen 1965, 561–63), but with due respect my late mentor, I must disagree. The physical evidence is simply not present in southeastern Tennessee, and the area's late (post-1830s) place in the settlement of the region does not fit with map evidence of a few old dogtrots dating from 1698 in Pennsylvania, 1739 in Maryland, 1783 in Virginia, 1784 in Middle Tennessee, and 1795 in North Carolina (Jordan and Kaups 1989, 179–96). The cultural geographer Gene Wilson found many dogtrot examples in Alabama (especially in the northern and central parts of the state) that far outnumber all other folk types combined (Wilson 1975, 32–43; Ferris 1980 and 1986; Wilson and Ferris 1989; Newton 1989, 498–99; Upton 1989, 146). Observing dogtrots in Middle Tennessee, Richard Hulan suggested that we should seek origins for the house type in the Bluegrass Basin of Kentucky, which was settled by "old-fashioned Virginians" (Hulan 1975, 42). While I appreciate Hulan's thinking, Kentucky simply does not appear to have quite that many dogtrots. Henry Glassie, one of America's foremost folklore experts, once thought that the dogtrot was an Appalachian variation of the hall-and-parlor house from the English-settled Tidewater region (Glassie 1968, 89–99). I disagreed with Glassie because if the hall-and-parlor was the progenitor house, then we should be seeing many more true dogtrots in the Lowland South, especially in the English-settled lowlands of Virginia, the Carolinas, and Georgia. But we do not find them there (Rehder 2004, 106–7).

The argument for Scandinavian origin is based on Martin Wright's early work and especially on the finely crafted arguments of Terry Jordan and Matti

Kaups's book *The American Backwoods Frontier* (Wright 1958; Jordan and Kaups 1989, 179–96, 249). Other than Jordan and Kaups, no one else has studied the dogtrot house sufficiently to reach a firm conclusion about its origin. Why won't I accept a Scandinavian origin and leave the subject alone? If we do so, I contend, then we should be able to connect it to the Swedes and Finns in the Delaware River Valley in about 1638–75. But we cannot, so the dots we seek to connect along the way through accepted avenues of diffusion are extremely scarce until we travel south and west beyond Appalachia. Maybe the idea of dogtrot architecture diffused southward from Pennsylvania but none of the physical evidence survived. This is obviously speculation, but it appears that vernacular scholars past and present can only speculate. We may never know how the dogtrot got to the South and how and why it diffused so widely beyond its suspected point of origin. We *can* say with certainty that the dogtrot is a wonderful example of a folk house of the American South. Sadly, however, it continues to disappear from the region's landscapes.

I-House

The I-house (Map 18), another step in the evolution of houses in the pen tradition, is a structure two full stories in height, two rooms wide, but only one room deep. The I-house can safely be described as ubiquitous because it is so widely distributed across the United States, extending from Pennsylvania to northern Florida, to southwestern Louisiana, to Texas, and all over the Midwest. It even appears out west in Utah, Washington, Oregon, and even California (Kniffen 1965, 553–57; Jordan 1985, 30–31; Glassie 1968, 64–69; Francaviglia 1979). Someone might describe it as a "two-over-two" kind of place or a double-pen that has doubled the number of rooms with a second story, but please don't refer to it that way.

The I-house got its name from Fred Kniffen, who observed houses of the type on rice farms in the southwestern prairies of Louisiana in the early 1930s. Kniffen discovered that the builder-owners of these houses were descendants of midwestern grain farmers who had migrated to southwestern Louisiana from Indiana, Illinois, and Iowa in the 1880s. Thus, Kniffen decided that the house type should be named for the first letter of each of those states. The name stuck and remains the conventional term in vernacular architecture scholarship today (Kniffen 1936, 179–93; Kniffen 1965, 553).

I-houses convey a special meaning to the rural landscape. Kniffen suggested that the house was a symbol of rural opulence and economic attainment in the Upland South and Appalachia, a region that has seen more than its share of poverty (Kniffen 1965, 555). James R. O'Malley, a former student of mine, proved Kniffen's opulence theory correct in a thorough study of I-houses in northeastern

The I-house, like this one in Blount County, is marked by a special formula of room arrangements: two stories tall, two rooms wide, and one room deep.

Tennessee. He discovered that 86 of his 113 sampled I-houses could be directly correlated to large landholdings characterized by gentle slopes and the best soils (O'Malley 1972, chap. 3; O'Malley 1977).

Construction methods for I-houses range from hewn logs, to rounded logs, to sawn lumber, to brick or stone. In a study of 50 I-houses located in Grainger, Knox, and Sevier counties, Karen Rehder found 41 constructed of framed sawn lumber, 8 of brick, and 1 of stone. However, she found no log examples (K. Rehder 1989). In a 1979 comprehensive survey of Union County, Vince Ambrosia found only 4 log I-houses, all with half-dovetail notches (Ambrosia 1979, 14).

In the 42-county survey of log structures in Tennessee, there were 443 log I-houses out of the total 2,589 houses, or 17.1 percent in the group. This came as a surprise to me. Back in 1978, Jim O'Malley and I wrote a paper titled "The Two-Story Log House in the Upland South" to draw attention to a little-known and what we thought was a very limited pattern in Appalachian folk architecture (O'Malley and Rehder 1978, 904–15). I had no idea that log-constructed I-houses could possibly be this abundant in Tennessee, but they are. Because of the massive weight of logs and the height to which they had to be lifted, the task usually required more workers than one family could provide. Like the community involvement in Amish barn raisings, it would appear that large log I-houses had to be constructed in stages using gang labor. Sometimes slave labor was employed, as was the case for the huge log building called Wynnewood, constructed in 1828 in Sumner County northeast of Nashville. (See the case study on Wynnewood in chapter 5.)

The map distribution for log I-houses in Tennessee is quite extensive. The range is from 1 to 93 with Hawkins County garnering 93 or 20.9 percent of the entire log I-house population of 443. Other East Tennessee counties—Washington, with 28 log I-houses (6.3 percent); Sevier, with 21 (4.7 percent); Knox, with 20 (4.5 percent); Hamblen, with 18 (4 percent); and Johnson, with 17 (3.8 percent)—show significant numbers. Also impressive are the numbers from Middle Tennessee and the Nashville Basin's counties of Marshall, with 36 occurrences (8.1 percent); Maury, with 28 (6.3 percent); Dekalb, with 27 (6.0 percent); and Davidson, with 25 (5.6 percent).

The place of origin for the I-house appears clearly to be the British Isles. While Terry Jordan found common distributions of I-houses in the Fennoscandian source area, he suggested a probable British origin for the I-house in America. For once, other scholars agreed that the I-house in the vast United States has a common European origin (Kniffen 1965, 555; Jordan 1985, 149; Pillsbury 1976; Pillsbury and Kardos 1970). Outside end chimneys are English traits both for the

I-houses come in all kinds of conditions. This one, converted into a barn and found in Marshall County south of Nashville, has a dogtrot breezeway entrance—but don't call it a dogtrot house. (Courtesy of the Tennessee Historical Commission.)

In 1982, this old homeplace in Fentress County at Frogge appeared to be declining much too fast. Amazingly, two decades later, the feeble house was still standing. (Courtesy of the Tennessee Historical Commission.)

English Tidewater region and England proper. Regarding Tennessee I-houses, the form, dimensions, end chimney placements, and other diagnostic features point conclusively to influences from the British Isles.

I-houses appear on the landscape in parts of Appalachia and all across Tennessee. Most homes have wood-frame and sawn-lumber construction. Brick I-houses are fairly common. There are reasons why log I-houses are unusual. Once the I-house became a symbol of rural attainment, some families were unlikely to build a log I-house if sawmill lumber or brick materials were available. For someone moving up socially and economically, a log house was not the proper symbol of opulence. Furthermore, two-story log I-houses were and still are difficult to build. However, once built, a log I-house could be quickly weatherboarded and given the appearance of a fine finished product. I know of several I-houses that were constructed in just that way.

Stone Houses in a Land of Logs: While the purpose of this book is to explore log buildings, I should note that some of Tennessee's oldest folk houses are built of stone. Stone I-houses—more common in Pennsylvania, Maryland, and Virginia—diminish in number as one travels southward to Tennessee, but there are some notable examples in the Volunteer State.

In 1974, the author discovered this much-lived-in I-house on the banks of the Tennessee River at Loudon. The Carmichael Inn was built around 1810 and served the traveling public at Blair's Ferry, the major river crossing in Loudon County.

The Gillespie stone house in the Limestone community in Greene County was built in 1792 for George Gillespie. It is said that a Quaker stonemason named Seth Smith from Lancaster, Pennsylvania, built the house. Historian Carroll Van West describes the house as follows: "[It] . . . has three first-floor rooms with no central hallway, an arrangement common in colonial Pennsylvania. . . . With its central chimney, the floor plan was similar to those used by German farmers on the Pennsylvania frontier and later on the Virginia frontier" (West 1995, 148; Tennessee Historical Commission 1996, 107). My take on the Gillespie place is that it is a large German three-room house of a type common to the Pennsylvania German hearth. The second floor is really much like an attic.

In east Knox County on Thorngrove Pike is the Ramsay house, a well-preserved home built in 1795–97 for Francis A. Ramsay, a wealthy planter and friend of William Blount and other early settlers. This simple design in the I-house tradition was the work of Thomas Hope, a British-trained architect who came to the area from Charleston, South Carolina (West 1995, 72).

In Claiborne County in the town of Tazewell is a stone house built in 1814–18 by an Irishman named William Graham, the community's first permanent merchant. With this house, Graham had a traditional shelter to remind him of his

Irish homeland. Tazewell was an important gateway to the famous Cumberland Gap, through which an estimated 300,000 settlers passed between 1775 and 1810 on their way to interior lands. Graham's thriving trading business in Tazewell allowed him to establish a permanent residence there. The Graham house has been the home of John Kivett, whose family has owned it since 1906 (Kivett 2001; Rehder 2004, 109).

Middle Tennessee boasts some exceptional stone houses, especially in the Nashville Basin. In Sumner County near Castalian Springs is the tiny, rectangular, two-pen stone house that Irishman Hugh Rogan (1747–1814) built in 1800 (Hankins 1995). The restored Rogan house was moved about five miles south to its present site at the Bledsoe Lick Historical Park, an outdoor museum. Two miles west on TN 25 is the massive Cragfont mansion built between 1798 and 1802 (and completed, some say, in 1811) for James Winchester, a prominent planter from Maryland. Winchester hired a group of Baltimore stonemasons and craftsmen to come to Tennessee just to construct the stone mansion. (West 1995, 315–16; Tennessee Historical Commission 1996, 241). If you choose to visit these two sites, also look for nearby Wynnewood, Tennessee's largest log structure (featured in chapter 5).

Stone I-houses can reflect a high level of opulence. Cragfont, located near Castalian Springs in Sumner County east of Gallatin, was built by Maryland craftsmen in 1798–1802 for James Winchester, a well-to-do Maryland planter.

FOUR-PEN HOUSE

The four-pen house (Map 19) has four rooms, divided by a central hallway, on each of two floors. The house is the ultimate structure in the evolutionary line of pens, and it is also the largest house type in the region, thus suggesting the highest level of opulence in this otherwise poor, rural part of America. Four-pen houses are usually constructed of framed sawn lumber, brick, or stone but are seldom built with logs. I-houses and smaller structures can be constructed with horizontal logs, but it is difficult to build a four-pen, two-story log house (O'Malley and Rehder, 1978). Even so, there are 21 four-pen log houses in the 42-county survey of 2,589 log houses, or 0.08 percent of the total. While the number is small, I am surprised that as many as 21 such log structures exist in the first place. The map pattern for these houses shows selective concentrations of two to four buildings in counties known to have limestone soils, large-sized farms, and old heritages in log work such as Washington, Sevier, Overton, and Davidson counties. Still, log four-pens are quite scarce. Beyond Tennessee, in parts of Virginia in the richly settled areas of the Great Valley all the way to Pennsylvania, there are dozens of four-pen houses that once served as inns for travelers. The homes are enormous and represent the supreme stratum for folk housing; still, few were ever built with logs (Rehder 2004, 110–11).

TWENTIETH-CENTURY BUNGALOWS AND BOX HOUSES

Log construction declined for folk housing in Southern Appalachia in the years between 1870 and 1920. Moreover, the pen tradition—at least in logs—began to weaken too. The bungalow (Map 20) and the box-house (Map 21) types materialized from a rural revolution in material culture that was an age of sawmill lumber (Morgan 1990, 98–107; Rehder 2004, 112–15). A front-facing gable is the primary diagnostic trait for a bungalow. Floor plans usually have three or more rooms arranged in a double line along the long axis of the house. While they may resemble a shotgun house, in Tennessee they should not be confused with that house type, which is found more frequently in southern cities and on rural landscapes throughout the Lower Mississippi Valley (Vlach 1986). Chimney or stovepipe placements can be almost anywhere on bungalows, which are built with framed balloon 2-by-4-inch studs with double walls and weatherboarded with horizontal sawn lumber. Bungalows are simple, easily built homes, but box houses can be even simpler and cheaper. The roof may be either a saddle roof or a pyramidal roof or even a high-hip design, but most have saddle roofs whose ridges run in the direction of the long axis.

Four-pen houses with log construction are extremely rare. This once opulent home near downtown Columbia in Maury County was razed in 1983. (Courtesy of the Tennessee Historical Commission.)

The box house, by my definition, is a square to slightly rectangular shaped four-room house with all four rooms on one floor, or "four on one." If rectangular, the gables are sideward facing. The chimney can appear anywhere. I disagree with others about the identity of box or "boxed" houses. John Morgan and Michael Ann Williams, both fine scholars, identify this house type by the thin board-and-batten construction (Morgan 1990, 98–107; Williams 1995, 70–74), but I think that the construction technique alone cannot identify a house type. In my view, the floor plan and gable position are more important. Box houses were typically built with board-and-batten construction, but I have seen them balloon framed and weatherboarded with horizontal boards. And I have seen them constructed with logs.

While my focus is on Tennessee's log buildings, I should explain board-and-batten construction here because you may have seen it and probably don't know much about it. Also, many buildings constructed in this way are rapidly

Log Houses

Log bungalow house types are a twentieth-century phenomenon. This one is found in Church Hill, Hawkins County.

disappearing from the landscape. Board-and-batten construction begins with a thin frame of sills, plates, and corner posts; this is covered with thick vertical planks. Boards 8 to 10 inches wide are nailed up first; then, smaller 2-inch-wide battens are nailed over the interstices between boards. The term "batten" recalls the old nautical saying "Batten down the hatches!" Between 1880 and 1940 board-and-batten construction became the primary way to construct cheap buildings, whether box houses, sheds, barns, or logging and coal-camp buildings (especially coal-camp houses). Board-and-batten construction was cheap and easy, and it arrived at an ideal time—that is, when logging arrived on the rural landscape. In that era, portable sawmilling operations visited farms, as the old agriculturally settled areas were running out of suitable trees for log construction.

It may seem unusual, but some bungalow and box houses *were* built with logs. The 42-county survey data reveals 70 log bungalows and 71 log box houses. Together they represent about 5 percent of the 2,589 log houses in the group. The maps for each type show a widespread pattern. Nashville's Davidson County has the largest share with 16 (22.8 percent) log bungalows and 27 (38 percent) log box houses. In East Tennessee, Hawkins County has 8 (11.2 percent) log box houses, Knox and Washington counties each have 6 (8.5 percent) log bungalows, and Roane County has 5 (7.1 percent) log bungalows. Dates of construction for some of the log bungalows were 1910 for 2 houses and 1924, 1927, and 1930 for 3 others. Most log box houses were built in the 1930s. These were "Depression houses" built with small-diameter, round pine logs and saddle corner notches; the logs were painted in some instances.

The resurgence of log houses during the Great Depression era meant two things. First, folks found that log construction was a cheaper and easier way to build shelter when skilled labor and money were in short supply. The two-pen log house my father-in-law built was a testament to a poor man's need for shelter for his young family in 1941. Second, some folks reverted to an old, nearly forgotten construction technique that used whole pine logs and notched the corners with saddle notches. The folk structures built in the 1930s and 1940s never seemed to reach the quality of workmanship of those from the nineteenth century. During hard times, necessity bred the reinvention of folk traits in log construction that afterwards disappeared when times got better.

The use of sawn lumber for twentieth-century building was monumental throughout the South. Bungalows and box houses clearly took advantage of available sawn lumber that allowed for expanded house dimensions with more rooms under roof. Construction was no longer restricted by the length and weight of logs, and the floor plans were no longer constrained by log pens. Thin walls allowed for more interior and exterior openings. Cheap and available materials in

This box house in Hawkins County was built in 1938 with saddle-notched round pine logs.

Log Houses

the form of sawn planks, machine-cut nails, window glass, and tin roofs meant a revolution in folk housing. But it would be the last.

MATERIALS OTHER THAN LOGS

While construction materials may be logs, stones, bricks, or sawn lumber with balloon or board-and-batten construction, genuine folk buildings are folk first, regardless of the materials from which they are constructed. So why have I spent so much time discussing folk log architecture in this book? My aim is to illustrate that buildings constructed of logs have dominated many of the best historic folk landscapes in Tennessee. Log structures serve as both a surrogate and an authoritative diagnostic indicator of folk culture through architecture. But at no point should you, in your own search for folk houses, be disappointed by thinking that a framed saddlebag or a stone I-house are meaningless because they were not built of logs.

Chapter 4

Log Barns and Outbuildings

Tennessee's rural landscapes are conspicuously marked with rustic barns and small outbuildings. Barns (Map 22) also follow an evolutionary pattern with modular units called cribs instead of pens because, as I commented earlier, "*Pens* are for people but *cribs* are for critters." Cribs normally progress from single-cribs to double-cribs to four-cribs to larger transverse-crib barns (Noble 1984, vol. 2; Schimmer and Noble 1984). Just about all barns and outbuildings have dirt floors except for granaries, which typically have raised, wooden floors. Most log outbuildings are rough-hewn and drafty, with interstices intentionally left open for drying purposes. Just as with folk log houses, these structures were built with hand tools—axes, adzes, froes, drawknives, and other woodworking implements. Similarly, such rural folk log structures date from the eighteenth, nineteenth, and twentieth centuries. Outbuildings are occasionally planned in different ways from houses, yet they have forms and floor plans that come from traditions passed down through the generations.

The typology of barns begins with cribs, with an evolutionary pattern proceeding as follows: single-crib, single-crib plus gear shed, double-crib, four-crib, and transverse-crib. Other barn types are forebay and cantilever. Small outbuildings include smokehouses, springhouses, root cellars, hog pens, chicken coops, granaries, blacksmith shops, and others. Beyond these are gristmills, log churches, and log schools. The myriad log outbuildings I have studied were built before the 1960s, and many were already in ruins when our historic buildings surveys were made 30 years ago. Some structures no longer exist because their functional value ceased. No one I know in Grainger County, for example, uses a log smokehouse with the original intent—to cure hog meat in salt and hickory smoke and then to store it. In fact, of the 26 log smokehouses that John Morgan, Joy Medford, and I had examined in Grainger County in 1978, only a single log smokehouse was still in use then, and by 2001 even it was gone (Rehder, Morgan, and Medford 1979, 77–79; Rehder 2004, 130).

SINGLE-CRIB BARN

A single-crib barn (Map 23) is a one-unit structure with either a square or rectangular shape. Single-cribs are rarely large: dimensions range from 6 feet for some of the smaller elevations to 25 feet on the larger cribs. The function of a crib is storage. A corncrib usually stores dry corn on the cob, but it may also be used as an animal stall or for any number of other storage purposes. Some single-cribs may also have an adjacent shelter for farm implements with an oversized, overhanging roof called a gear shed. Not all single-cribs have the gear shed, but storage and protection functions are consistent with this type of barn.

For single-crib barns, the Tennessee survey data of 42 counties is rich. Of 1,619 log barns and outbuildings, 374 are single-cribs (23 percent). The map pattern shows the largest concentrations in the Ridge and Valley and Blue Ridge physiographic regions in East Tennessee. In Union County, 62 (16.5 percent) are single-cribs. Hawkins County has 48 (12.8 percent). Nearby, Grainger County has 21 (5.6 percent). Forty-seven (12.5 percent) are found in the mountain county of Johnson in the northeast corner of the state—the location of the Watauga River Valley and the old settlement hearth. The only other rich single-crib county is Giles with 29 (7.7 percent) such barns. Giles County is located on the southern edge of the Nashville Basin and southern Highland Rim area about 65 miles south of Nashville.

SINGLE-CRIB WITH GEAR SHED

A way to increase the functional size of a single-crib is to add a gear shed to the side (Map 24). Looking a bit like a frontier carport, the gear shed is open-sided and supported by posts and shares a common roof ridge with the main crib. Wagons, plows, and other farm implements are stored under the shed for protection from the weather. In the 42-county survey, there were 113 single-crib and gear shed log buildings out of 1,619, or about 7 percent. My mapped data show that the three richest counties were Hawkins with 40 (35.3 percent), Knox with 17 (15 percent), and Sevier with 14 (12.3 percent); all are in East Tennessee. In Middle Tennessee, Jackson County on the rough edge of the Eastern Highland Rim had 12 (10.6 percent).

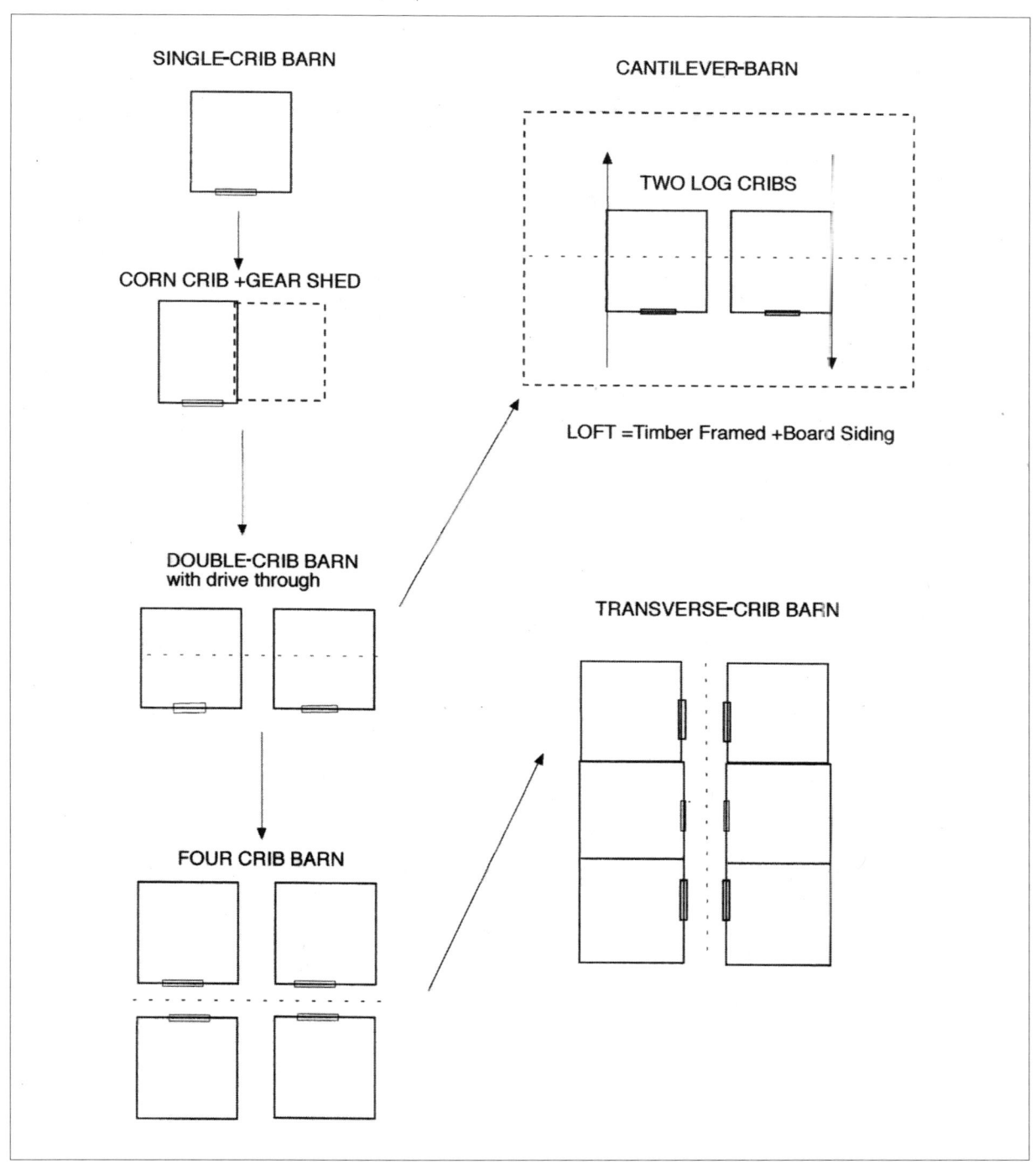

The evolution of barns begins with a single-crib. It then proceeds to the single-crib with a gear shed to double-crib barns, four-crib barns, and transverse-crib barns. Cantilever barns are usually derived from double-crib barns. (Sources: Kniffen 1965; Jordan and Kaups 1989; Jordan-Bychkov 1998; Rehder 2004.)

A typical single-crib barn has a front-facing gable and Alpine roof projection. When used for corn storage, the single-crib is called a corn crib. This crib's location in West Tennessee's Hardeman County demonstrates the wide diffusion of traditional folk architecture. (Courtesy of the Tennessee Historical Commission.)

DOUBLE-CRIB BARN

Early on, Appalachian farmers decided that a single-crib could be doubled into two-crib barns by adding another crib to the side of the first one. The double-crib barn (Map 25) features two cribs separated by an open passage but covered with a common ridgepole saddle roof. Double-crib barns thus resemble dogtrot houses, but the two structure types do not positively correlate geographically in the Upland South. However, my late friend Terry Jordan, a cultural geographer, found close correlations between double-pen houses and double-crib barns in Sweden (Jordan 1985, 146, 149). Double-crib barns come in a variety of shapes and sizes and serve various functions. Like a single-crib, double-cribs can be square or rectangular. They can vary in size from 4 by 8 feet per crib to 18 by 24 feet but are rarely any larger.

Some double-cribs have a simple saddle roof that follows the long axis; others have a projecting "Alpine" roof that is oriented front to back over the short axis of the structure, forming a gable-oriented roofline. The Alpine roof projection on double-crib barns is found more frequently in the northern half of Appalachia than in the southern half. As I suggested in my book *Appalachian Folkways*, I believe that the Alpine roof detail came from Germanic Europe via the Pennsylvania German culture hearth (Rehder 2004, 119–20).

The single-crib with a gear shed, like this one in Grainger County, combines a single-crib (left) with an open shed (right) for implement or gear storage. (Courtesy of the Tennessee Historical Commission.)

In the Tennessee data analysis, 362 (22.3 percent) of 1,619 barns and outbuildings are double-crib barns. These are widely distributed across the state and range on a county basis from 1 to 72. No particular region dominates the map pattern. Northeast Tennessee's Johnson County has the most, with 72 (19.8 percent) of the 362 double-crib barns. Hawkins has 55 (15.1 percent), Sevier has 53 (14.6 percent), Giles has 25 (6.9 percent), and Lincoln has 23 (6.3 percent). Other representative counties are Jackson, with 13 (3.6 percent) double-cribs; Union, with 12 (3.3 percent); Cannon, with 11 (3.0 percent); and Hardeman and Blount, with 10 (2.7 percent) each.

The counties in West Tennessee deserve closer attention, so I am going to show the data a bit differently by calculating the percentage of double-cribs to all log outbuildings for each county. Eleven (or 36.6 percent) of all of Cannon County's 30 log outbuildings are double-cribs. Ten (or 31.2 percent) of Hardeman's 32 log outbuildings are double-cribs. In the Highland Rim area, Jackson's 13 double-cribs out of 58 log structures represent 22.4 percent of that county's total. In the southern part of the Nashville Basin and southern edge of the Highland Rim country, Lincoln's 23 double-cribs of 62 log barns and outbuildings represents 37 percent of the county total. Proportionally within each county, these are noteworthy figures.

The abundance of double-crib barns throughout the state, but especially in East Tennessee's Johnson and Hawkins counties, reflects three factors. First,

The double-crib barn has two cribs and an open drive-through passage between them. Located in Clay County, this saddle-roof example was an accidental discovery described in chapter 1.

As this example from Hawkins County shows, some double-crib barns may feature an orientation in which the roof line parallels the crib's long axis. Such structures appear to have a greater connection with German barns in Pennsylvania and can be traced to those in Alpine Europe. (Courtesy of the Tennessee Historical Commission.)

double-crib hay barns, sometimes described as "pole barns," became popular in the 1930s and especially after World War II, so such structures are part of the catch. Second, John Morgan and his surveyors from Emory and Henry College were so thorough in their work that their catch rate was exceptionally high. When Morgan's crews, more meticulous than most, examined the interiors of lumber-sided barns, they found double-cribs serving as foundations. Third, I erroneously interpreted a number of barns as double-cribs because log cribs can be used on other barn types for foundations. If I were to reexamine the data, some double-crib barns might be reclassified as cantilever barns because such buildings have dual log-crib underpinnings. To sum up: few surveyors are as thorough as Morgan's people; not every data analyst (including me) can be completely accurate; and data sets surely have flaws. Still, I believe that Johnson and Hawkins counties dominate the single- and double-crib barn picture because the area is so very rich in log buildings in general (Rehder 2004, 120–21). I should add that other counties have a strong showing when it comes to double-cribs. These include East Tennessee's Sevier County with 53 and Union with 12. Very impressive also are the Middle Tennessee counties of Giles with 25 double-cribs and adjacent Lincoln County with 23.

FOUR-CRIB BARN

The four-crib barn (Map 26) represents a larger landscape expression with a crib on each of the four corners. The entryways lead to open passages crossing at the center to separate the four cribs. A gabled roof covers the entire structure. The international folklorist Henry Glassie described the evolution of the four-crib barn and its transformation into a transverse-crib barn this way: "The Tennessee farmer found himself in need of a large barn. . . . He built a pair of double-crib barns facing each other, roofed the whole, and had a four-crib barn. As it was built, the four-crib barn developed its own symmetry, one of its two passageways was blocked off to provide additional stabling, and this painfully neat evolutionary sequence resulted in the transverse-crib barn" (Glassie 1968, 89). I like Glassie's thinking, but in my study of Appalachian four-crib barns, I've observed that the four-cribs were sometimes constructed and covered all at the same time. Some four-crib barns are not very old, with many dating between late 1880s and the 1940s.

A wonderful example of a four-crib barn readily accessible to visitors can be found at a place I've already mentioned, the Noah "Bud" Ogle farm complex in the Great Smoky Mountains National Park above and east of Gatlinburg. (See chapter 3 for directions.) The barn's four cribs, anchoring the corners, measure just less than 11 feet (between 10 feet 6 inches and 10 feet 11 inches) on each side. The open passages measure 11 feet 2 inches for the east-west passage and 6 feet 9 inches for the north-south passage. Built sometime after 1879, this unique and well-preserved four-crib still contains some of the original chestnut.

Log four-crib barns in my survey data account for just 54 (3.3 percent) examples out of 1,619 log outbuildings. Four counties have a strong showing, but the mapped pattern is not very clear. Sevier County had the most with 13 (24 percent). Jackson County had 8 (14.8 percent), Giles had 7 (12.9 percent), and Union county had 5 (9.2 percent). Hawkins had 3 and Bradley and Overton counties had 2 barns each. I know of a few more here and there, with 1 each in Putnam, Maury, White, Hancock, Johnson, Marion, Chester and Cannon counties.

TRANSVERSE-CRIB BARN

Another method of barn expansion is to join three or four cribs on each side of a central passage, creating a transverse-crib barn (Map 27). The large barn may be from 50 to 90 feet long, with a single central passage. The multiple cribs on each

In 1958, the four-crib barn at the Noah "Bud" Ogle place in the Great Smoky Mountains National Park was in such good condition that it required little restoration beyond the shake roofing that came later. (Library of Congress, Prints and Photographs Division, Historical American Buildings Survey, HABS TN-123. Photo by Jack E. Boucher, Nov. 1958.)

Transverse-crib barns have three or more cribs on either side of an open passageway. This one with saddle-V notches was an accidental discovery near Monterey in Putnam County.

side are its best diagnostic trait. The cribs are used for different purposes: some are corncribs to store livestock feed, while others are used as stables for farm mules, horses, or other animals. As Glassie indicated in the quotation above, the transverse-crib evolved in concept and in actuality from the four-crib barn. Both the four-crib and transverse-crib are considered original American barn types but with linkages through the single- and double-crib barns to Western Europe (Glassie 1968, 89, 228; Jordan 1985, 113, 149; Jordan 1998, 1–31).

The mapped data in the 42-county survey indicates sparse appearances of log transverse-crib barns with 52 of 1,619 outbuildings, or 3.2 percent. Somehow, I expected more. Giles County had 9 (17.3 percent of the 52-barn total), Jackson County had 8 (15.3 percent), and Sevier and Hawkins counties each had 5 (9.6 percent). Johnson, Marion, Van Buren, Cannon, and Hardeman counties have 3 transverse crib barns each. It is entirely possible that other four-crib and transverse-crib barns had been covered over with sawn lumber weatherboarding and thus escaped detection from the surveyors. It is entirely possible that other transverse-crib barns exist in counties that have not been surveyed.

CANTILEVER BARN

One of the most striking barns on the Appalachian landscape is the cantilever barn (Map 28), a structure marked by large beams that support a large hayloft under which log cribs (usually two of them) serve as foundation units. A cantilever barn begins with stone footers or foundations set at each corner of the cribs. The flat stones level the cribs and keep the logs off the ground to prevent moisture and insect damage. Logs that have been either hewn square or left in the round are notched and placed horizontally atop each other and erected with four to eight courses per side to create each crib. Crib sizes range from 13 feet to about 24 feet on a side. (The largest barn of which I am aware was built in 1880 by Thomas DeArnold Wilson McMahan in Sevier County and features cribs measuring 18 feet by 24 feet.) The cribs are open air with no chinking and have wooden doors or gates cut into them. The barns have dirt floors, and most cribs have been used as animal stalls or corncribs. Some barns had a threshing floor, indicative of the time when wheat was an important crop in the Ridge and Valley region. Large cantilever beams, ranging from 30 to 40 feet long and from 10 to 18 inches thick, are the key diagnostic feature of the cantilever barn (Moffett and Wodehouse 1993, 3–4, 8–9; Rehder 2004, 124–28).

In Tennessee's cantilever barns, like this one in Sevier County, only the cribs are constructed with logs. The loft is timber-framed and weatherboarded. (Courtesy of the Tennessee Historical Commission.)

A cantilever barn's foundation consists of two log cribs, as shown in this example from Cades Cove in the Great Smoky Mountains National Park (Blount County).

In a survey of cantilever barns in East Tennessee, architectural historians Marian Moffett and Lawrence Wodehouse discovered 316 log barns they classified as cantilever barns. Of these, 291 had double-crib foundations. Modifying the terminology of Moffett and Wodehouse's typology and based on their count, we can account for 161 two-crib, double-cantilever barns; 112 two-crib, single-cantilever barns; 18 two-crib barns with single *and* double cantilevers (Moffett and Wodehouse inexplicably called this a "half-double cantilever"); 12 single-crib, double-cantilever barns; 8 four-crib cantilevered barns; and 5 unclassified (Moffett and Wodehouse 1993, 9). The prevailing type is the two-crib, double-cantilever barn, which accounts for 161 (51 percent) of the 316 barns in the Moffett-Wodehouse survey. Diagnostic traits of this dominant barn are (1) two log cribs for the foundation support and (2) two sets of cantilevers that support the overhanging loft on all four sides. Imagine two square-shaped cribs set side by side. Across the tops of both cribs are large wooden beams laid across at right angles in both directions. The beams extend well beyond the dimensions of the cribs, so that the structure appears to be extremely top heavy with a huge hayloft. Above the framed loft is a large saddle roof whose ridge follows the long axis. The tall outside walls of the loft are weatherboarded with sawmill siding (Rehder 2004, 124–25).

Another cantilever barn type is the two-crib, single-cantilever barn that accounts for another 112 structures (36 percent) out of the 316 total in the Moffett-Wodehouse survey. The barn has the same two log cribs supporting the loft, but the loft's gable ends are flush with the log cribs underneath. Thus, the long cantilever feature only operates in a single direction along one axis of the structure (Moffett and Wodehouse 1993, 9).

The cantilever barns in the Moffett-Wodehouse survey overwhelmingly made use of half-dovetail notches: 208 (67 percent) out of 310 log structures. Barns with V notches accounted for 58 structures (19 percent) and 35 (11 percent) had square notches. Nine of the barns had a mixture of half-dovetail and V notches (Moffett and Wodehouse 1993, 4). One of the problems in barn-type identification is that weatherboards cover the outer sides of many log barns. In the field we may see an enormous weatherboarded barn with a huge loft, but the weatherboarding may obscure the two small cribs underneath that support the entire structure.

I have had some problems with the inventory numbers of cantilever barns in Tennessee. Having mapped and analyzed the 42-county Tennessee Historical Commission survey data, including the numbers for Blount and Sevier counties, I found a total of only 195 cantilever barns (as opposed to the 316 in the Moffett-Wodehouse survey). Sevier County clearly has the lion's share with 150 of the 195 barns (an impressive 76.9 percent), but neighboring Blount County shows only 12 barns. Johnson County has 9 cantilever barns; Bradley has 6; Meigs has 4; and Morgan has 1.

Other than for Sevier and Blount counties, I think I can explain the distribution patterns for the other counties. Johnson County, a mountain county in northeastern Tennessee in the Watauga culture hearth subregion, has a quantity of well-built, small cantilevered outbuildings, which may account for the focus

Surveys in Sevier County yielded 183 cantilever barns in 1984 and 150 in 1991. Despite declining numbers, some barns remain protected.

of some cantilevered barns. Bradley and Meigs counties, in the Ridge and Valley region, are located on the old main route for transportation, communication, and settlement migrations down-valley from Pennsylvania and points in between. They would have been in a direct line to receive traits, such as barn concepts and patterns that diffused from Pennsylvania. The one barn in Morgan County on the Cumberland Plateau might be an anomaly; however, German surnames and the name of the county seat, Wartburg, indicate the presence of German settlers (Rehder 2004, 126–27). As I'll explain more fully in a moment, I believe that the cantilever barn has European origins and came to Tennessee from the German culture hearth in southeastern Pennsylvania.

The uncertainty in the numbers occurs mainly in the data for Blount and Sevier counties. For Sevier County, Moffett and Wodehouse's survey showed a high concentration of 183 cantilever barns, while the Tennessee Historical Commission's survey showed 150, which is not a discrepancy sufficient to cause much concern. However, in my analysis of the THC survey data, I found only 12 log cantilever barns in adjacent Blount County, as opposed to 104 cantilever barns, 98 of them with log cribs, for the same county in the Moffett-Wodehouse survey. Why such a difference? One explanation may be that I missed a number of covered log barns in my image analysis in the archives.*

The two exceptional counties, Blount and Sevier, accounted for 287 of the 316 barns (or 90 percent) of the barns in the Moffett-Wodehouse study of 11 Tennessee counties. This led those authors to speculate, and I am sure erroneously, that cantilever barns were indigenous to this part of East Tennessee. *Indigenous*, in the anthropological sense means native to an area, original, invented *in situ*, on site. Try as I might, I could never convince Marian Moffett and Larry Wodehouse (now both deceased) that the true origins of the cantilever barn could be traced to Old World European source areas (Moffett and Wodehouse 1993, xv, 86–114; Rehder 2004, 126).

The principle of cantilever construction is not really unique. In Tennessee, we observe it in other small outbuildings as well as in large barns. The cantilever barn here is a variation of the forebay or Pennsylvania barn. I believe that the cantilever log barn originated in Europe and came to America with German immigrants who entered through Philadelphia and began a settlement migration from the southeastern Pennsylvania German hearth in the 1700s. Ideas of barn construction diffused down the Great Valley route in the Ridge and Valley

---

*Editor's Note: An article by John Morgan detailing research on log barns in Blount County indicates a total even higher than that of the Moffett-Wodehouse survey: approximately 121 log cantilever barns (Morgan and Lynch 1984, 90–98). Unfortunately, in part because of Professor Rehder's death before this book went into production, the disparity in data remains unresolved.

physiographic region as German immigrants, along with Scotch-Irish, English, and others, made their way southward, generation by generation, along the Philadelphia Wagon Road and other routes to settle Southern Appalachia. Naturally, over time, barns were modified. We know for certain that barns became smaller as settlers traveled north to south from Pennsylvania to Tennessee and into Alabama and Georgia. Large barn size is believed to have been related to the need to shelter livestock in colder northern climates while smaller barn size in the South could be correlated with open range stock raised in milder climatic regimes. The milder southern winters made large barns for livestock shelters unnecessary (Kniffen 1965; Morgan 1997; Rehder 2004, 126–27).

What were the circumstances that brought the cantilever barn to Tennessee? Although we have somewhat limited landscape evidence, we can still connect the dots of cantilever barn occurrences in Tennessee, Virginia, and Pennsylvania back to origins in Europe (Morgan 1997; Ensminger 1992). John Morgan has found noteworthy cantilever barn examples in Virginia, so the patterns linking Pennsylvania and Tennessee are much clearer over the traceable route and over much of the temporal range. Suddenly, however, we see an explosion of cantilever barns all over Sevier and Blount counties, Tennessee, in the 1880s and 1890s. Moffett and Wodehouse stated that more than half of the 316 cantilever barns in their survey dated to this quite narrow time frame (Moffett and Wodehouse 1993, 16). It is astounding but not out of the question that a resurgence of log cantilever barns could emerge under the right conditions (Rehder 2004, 125–27).

Strangely, something encouraged such a change in folk culture, and I am still uncertain what it was. Perhaps the cantilever barn grew out of (1) a need for larger barns with huge hay lofts for the cattle herds that developed in the post–Civil War period, (2) the possibility that skilled builders may have come south after the Civil War to either settle in eastern Tennessee or ply their barn-building trades here, (3) the emergence of skilled "knowers" among farmer/builders, (4) the appearance of folk who by word of mouth spread the idea that a cantilever barn was a "must have" (as in "keeping up with the Joneses"), and/or (5) the post–Civil War emergence of sawmills and sawn lumber for hayloft construction. These factors might explain the framed hayloft part of the equation. But what about the logs? I believe that the continued use of log construction for cribs was carried through by traditional ways of building, but in these instances the strong log cribs were relegated to foundation supports (Rehder 2004, 127).

The idea of the cantilever barn was a folk trait rekindled in a small part of East Tennessee over the course of about a decade in the late nineteenth century. I do not think that the cantilever barn was ever indigenous to the area or to the time. Perhaps the cantilever idea had been incubating in other areas and at other times, but it was an idea whose time had come when it flourished suddenly in Sevier and Blount counties (Rehder 2004, 126–28). We can understand the importance of key "knowers," builders, and teachers of the culture, and this followed a migration of a trend if not a people. The cantilever barn was not indigenous to any part of America, but it became a profound diagnostic trait in Appalachia that can be traced back to Europe and remains a wonderful symbol of our folk cultural heritage.

SMALL OUTBUILDINGS

The renowned folklorist Henry Glassie once described the typical Appalachian small outbuilding this way: "It has a rectangular floor plan, consistent with German and Scotch-Irish traditions, a regular double pitch roof, and a door in one gable end. . . . Although not always present, its most distinguishing feature is a projecting roof, constructed on a cantilever principle typical of Pennsylvania German construction" (Glassie 1964, 1–6).

Small outbuildings have a much greater variety in their functions than in their forms. Similar-looking buildings can be smokehouses, root or apple houses, springhouses, dairy or milk houses, washhouses, and other specialized storage structures or animal enclosures built mostly for protection purposes. While most small outbuildings have one level, others may have two levels. Some are built into steep slopes with a stone root cellar and a wooden upper level. A unique two-level subtype has cantilevered projections for a small porch between bottom and upper cribs and a cantilevered roof projection as well. The form of a typical small outbuilding is a single-crib, measuring about 12 by 14 feet, with a square or rectangular shape. Diagnostic traits are the front-facing gable and Alpine roof overhang built at the gable entrance to provide shelter to the doorway.

SMOKEHOUSES

The smokehouse (Map 29) was vital to a culture that raised hogs in a "hog meat and corn pone" subsistence economy. Structurally, smokehouses are small outbuildings with a front-facing gable and a projecting roof that overhangs the door. Used for salting and smoking meat, they could once be found on just about every farm. In 1978, John Morgan, Joy Medford, and I analyzed 26 log smokehouses in a historic buildings survey of Grainger County, Tennessee. We investigated the log smokehouse as part of the folk architecture, and we searched for traditional functions and alternative uses for them. The smallest smokehouse measured 7 feet 10 inches by 10 feet 3 inches; the largest smokehouse was 16 feet 9 inches square. Out of 26 buildings, 24 structures (or 92 percent) had the diagnostic roof overhang at the gable entrance. Smokehouses with half-dovetail notches dominated the construction with 19 occurrences (73 percent), while 6 buildings (23 percent) were V-notched and 1 was square-notched (Rehder, Morgan, and Medford 1979, 77). Imagine our disappointment when we found only a single log smokehouse still functioning as originally intended. In the fall of 2001, I returned to Grainger County to do additional fieldwork and discovered that this last functioning smokehouse, once operated by a Mr. Longmire, had disappeared (Rehder 2004, 129–30).

When smokehouses were common, the method for preserving meat was to coat it in salt and allow the meat to absorb as much of the salt as possible over the course of six or more weeks. When hogs were slaughtered in the late fall, prepared cuts of the meat were placed on a salting board, in a box, or in a trough made from a hollowed-out poplar tree trunk. Sometimes, salting boards two to three feet wide were wedged between logs inside the unchinked smokehouse and rubbed with salt there. Meat cuts in salting boxes or a trough were left to absorb more salt over the six- to eight-week curing period. Ham, bacon, and shoulder pieces would be strung up on poles that spanned the length of the structure about five feet above the ground. A smoldering fire in hickory wood chips was then set in the center of the smokehouse's dirt floor. The smoking process lasted about a week, after which the meat would be ready to eat (Rehder, Morgan, Medford

At one time, nearly every working farm in Tennessee had a smokehouse for salting, smoking, and storing hog meat. They are now used for storing garden tools and assorted junk. This example is from Johnson County.

1979, 79; Rehder 2004, 129–30, 212–16; Fox 2001). When the slaughtering-salting-smoking processes ended, the building became the storehouse for cured meat for the next year.

Examination of the 42-county data revealed 377 log smokehouses out of 1,619 log outbuildings, or 23.2 percent—a strong showing. The map patterns reveal two concentrations. Giles County on the southwestern edge of the Nashville Basin led the group with 57 smokehouses, or 15.1 percent. (My book *Appalachian Folkways* includes a graphic description of hog killing and meat preparation by my former student Todd Fox; it is not surprising that Todd's family story comes from Giles County [Fox 2001; Rehder 2004, 212–16].) In East Tennessee's Ridge and Valley Province, Hawkins County had 44 log smokehouses (11.6 percent), Blount had 42 (11.1 percent), Union had 36 (9.5 percent), Grainger had 26 (6.8 percent), Knox had 24 (6.3 percent), and Jefferson and Washington counties each had 10 (2.7 percent). Sevier County, which is located in both the Ridge and Valley and Blue Ridge provinces, had 33 smokehouses (8.7 percent), while Johnson County, a Blue Ridge county in the northeast corner of Tennessee, had 25 (6.6 percent). To my knowledge, there are no log smokehouses still functioning as intended in the surveyed counties in East Tennessee.

TWO-LEVEL CANTILEVERED LOG OUTBUILDINGS

I have discovered a unique small outbuilding subtype that has two levels—one above the other. Even more unusual is the use of cantilevers to support a porch between the two levels. The building also features a cantilevered roof projection, a common trait among small outbuildings with a front-facing gable. A good example is found on the Layman (perhaps once spelled Lehmann) farm in Sevier County located on the limestone-rich north slope of English Mountain in an area settled by Germans in 1787 called the "Old Dutch Settlement." This two-story smokehouse is 12 feet long by 9 feet wide and measures 12 feet from the ground to the roof ridge. At this height, each level is 6 feet high. The building is constructed with half-dovetail notches on good, heart pine logs and dates to about 1890 or perhaps a little earlier.

This site and similar ones made me curious about the spatial and temporal context for these small, double-level log buildings. Let's connect the dots from north to south. In Tennessee, we begin in the state's northeastern-most county, Johnson, with a two-story, cantilevered log springhouse on the Jesse Gambill farm. It was built around 1880. Next is the "Swaggerty Blockhouse" in Cocke County, where (as detailed in chapter 1) graduate student David Mann surprised everyone with the confirmed date of 1860 for a structure (which is not really a blockhouse) that was long believed to have been built in 1787. Next are the

The use of cantilevers was not exclusive to barns. This rare two-level smokehouse with half-dovetail notches on pine logs was built in the 1880s in the "Old Dutch (Deutsch) Settlement" in eastern Sevier County.

Layman and Schraeder sites in east Sevier County on the north slope of English Mountain; they are on the same road and less than a mile apart. In 2005, Dennis Layman told me that his building was "about a hundred years old," and indeed, in 1991, Robbie Jones estimated a date of about 1890 for the structure in the THC's survey of Sevier County. An identical building on the nearby Schraeder farm dates to around 1885. Farther south but still in Sevier County is the Ingles Hollow site with another fine example (now gone) of a cantilevered two-level small outbuilding that Jones dated at around 1875. (Incidentally, the Ingles Hollow site once had a large cantilevered barn that is also gone.) To the south and west in the Middle Settlements of Blount County are two more two-level structures, one of which is dated circa 1875 in John Morgan's survey.

So, here we have several two-story cantilevered log structures that follow a geographic pattern from Johnson County to Cocke, Sevier, and Blount counties. The buildings date from around 1860 to about 1890 but not much later. This period of extraordinary log construction happens to coincide with that of cantilever barn construction in East Tennessee. I believe that both the barns and the smaller outbuildings have the same origins, going back to the German Culture Hearth of southeastern Pennsylvania and thence to Alpine Europe with its forebay and cantilever barns. It is only fitting that we now see it evidenced by these much smaller but fascinating cantilever log outbuildings.

Now gone, this two-level smokehouse, nearly identical to the one shown in the photo on page 100 was located in Ingles Hollow in western Sevier County. (Courtesy of the Tennessee Historical Commission.)

SPRINGHOUSES

In frontier settlement, a nearby clean-water source came first. Integral to first effective settlement were soil, access, slope, and wooded acreage, but none appear to have been nearly as important as drinking water. Springs have always been the primary source for water even with creeks and rivers in the area. Providing clear, clean drinking water, the chosen spring was as important to life on the family homestead as the cooking hearth was. A cool-water spring, enjoyable on hot summer days, needed protection from the elements with a structure called a springhouse (Map 30). This outbuilding protected the drinking water source from contamination by leaves, sediment, dead animals, and other debris. It was also a crude but efficient refrigerator, inside of which milk, butter, and perishables other than meat were kept in troughs of cool spring water (Rehder 2004, 130–32).

The shapes and sizes of springhouses are much like those of smokehouses: roughly 6 by 10 feet to as large as 10 by 16 feet. They almost always feature a stone foundation around the spring. Walls can be built of logs or framed sawn wood. The roof, once made of wooden shakes, may now have a galvanized corrugated metal covering. The Alpine roof overhang on the gable-end entrance is a feature highly characteristic of Appalachian small outbuildings. One or two

A good spring was an especially important element in the choice of sites for settling the frontier. With a stone foundation and cooling troughs below and a log unit above, a springhouse —this one is found in Hawkins County— protected the vital water source and provided the farm with a pioneer refrigerator.

stone troughs measuring 2–3 feet wide by 6–8 feet long are filled with cold spring water. Many springhouses have raised stone levels that serve as shelves. The floor of the springhouse is shaped with flat stones.

Numerous springhouses in Appalachia are constructed of framed, sawn wood or stone, but a few are built with logs. In our survey of log buildings, there were a total of 34 log springhouses, the majority of them located in East Tennessee from Blount County northward to the Virginia state line. Of the 34 log springhouses in the data set, Union County had eight (23.5 percent), Hawkins had seven (20.5 percent), Johnson County had four (11.7 percent), and Blount, Grainger and Sevier each had three. Dekalb, Hardeman, Knox, Maury, Sequatchie, and Washington counties each had one. As scattered as they appear, all were located in areas with limestone geology where springs are preferred over wells for drinking water even today. With the mere mention of springhouses in the field, I still get a smile from folks telling me that they know the meaning of good-tasting, cold, spring water. In one famous instance, however, spring water has been used for a somewhat different purpose: Beginning in 1866, Jasper "Jack" Daniel in Moore County incorporated it into his recipe for a fine Tennessee sipping whiskey. The world-famous Jack Daniel's Distillery in Lynchburg still prides itself on the quality of the water used in its sour mash whiskey (Tolley 1998, 467).

ROOT CELLARS, APPLE HOUSES, AND CANNING HOUSES

The outbuilding complex on some mountain farms may also include root cellars, apple houses, and canning cellars/houses. They provide the food storage that ordinarily does not apply to smokehouses and springhouses. Potatoes, apples and other fruit, and canned and dried vegetables require dry, cool storage that these small specialty buildings provide. While their names imply specialization, apple houses and potato houses do not exclusively store apples and potatoes; they can be canning cellars for other fruits and vegetables. These small structures are similar to smokehouses and springhouses in shape and size. They often have the projected diagnostic roof and like the others feature a gable-end door opening. The primary difference with cellar buildings is that they have a stone cellar built into a hillside. Some buildings have a second-floor storage room built of logs or framed, sawn wood above the stone cellar. The best diagnostic characteristic of the building is the stone cellar, which is only partially underground. Inside are long shelves lined with glass jars filled with vegetables, fruits, and meats.

The best concentration of these small cellar-buildings is found in the mountainous Blue Ridge and Ridge and Valley areas of northeastern Tennessee. In the survey, there are only nine log structures of this type. Johnson County in the

Root cellars, canning cellars, and apple houses have a stone semi-subterranean cellar for long-term food storage. The upper portion, constructed of logs or framed sawn wood, became another storage facility. This example was photographed in Johnson County. (Courtesy of the Tennessee Historical Commission.)

Log Barns and Outbuildings

northeastern corner of the state has four (44.4 percent); Hawkins County, a little southwest of that, has four (44.4 percent); and Marshall County in Middle Tennessee has just one (11.1 percent) log canning cellar. Almost all root and canning outbuildings have the stone cellar, but many more appear on the landscape with framed, sawn-wood superstructures for the upper level. It is in the Watauga hearth culture region, where Johnson and Hawkins counties are located, that we find solid concentrations of these small log and framed outbuildings used as food storage cellars.

OTHER LOG BUILDINGS

Tennessee's farmsteads clearly had other structures in the outbuilding complex: chicken coops, hog pens, granaries, blacksmith shops, and numerous other enclosures and storage structures. Beyond the farms, there were also rural log churches and log schools.

CHICKEN COOPS, GRANARIES, AND BLACKSMITH SHOPS

Farmers kept chickens in elevated chicken coops to protect the birds from foxes and snakes. Coops had low, single-slanted roofs that were higher in front; doors were on the gable sides (Rehder 2004, 133–34). I have limited data on only 10 log coops. Of these, 5 (50 percent) are in Giles County on the southwestern corner of the Nashville Basin, and Blount, Cannon, Chester, Jackson, and Van Buren counties each have 1 log coop. That 5 coops are found in Giles County is significant to me. A tradition-rich county, Giles stands out for its abundance of old log structures. It is akin to East Tennessee's Johnson, Hawkins, Grainger, and Union counties in having so many significant log building types as well as high numbers of them. If it were not located about 365 miles away, one might think that Giles County is somewhere in Upper East Tennessee.

Granaries (Map 31) are larger than smokehouses and have gable-end doors. Their key diagnostic traits are their plank floors and their unusual height above ground. The first feature meant that the grain (any grain other than corn, which was kept in corncribs) could be kept dry; the height was believed to protect the grain from vermin. The survey data reveals nine log granaries. Five are found in Blount County (55.5 percent) and two are in Knox County (22.2 percent) in East Tennessee. Middle Tennessee's Giles County and West Tennessee's Hardeman County have one each.

Like this one in Grainger County, granaries were built with tighter walls and raised floors and were used for storing grain other than corn. (Courtesy of the Tennessee Historical Commission.)

Log blacksmith shops are scarce. This one in Union County is one of the oldest documented log buildings in Tennessee. Dendrochronology determined a date of 1793.

The blacksmith shop or smithy (Map 32) is a very low, ground-hugging structure. The few log ones have their own special diagnostic traits: a height under 6 feet at the edge of the eaves and wide openings 6–8 feet long and 1–2 feet or even 3 feet high on the long axis of the structure, but still low to the ground. The blacksmith shop also has a rectangular shape, a gable-end door, and a bare earthen floor. The smithy's wide openings on the long axis of the structure are especially diagnostic because a blacksmith required daylight to illuminate his work, fresh air to feed the bellows, and room to maneuver large metal objects that were sometimes fed into the building through these low wide windows on the long sides of the structure. There are not many original log blacksmith shops left on the landscape. Only four built of logs appear in the 42-county survey, one each in Grainger, Jefferson, Johnson, and Union counties. The one in Union County is an outstanding example because of its age: dendrochronology dates it to 1793 (Reding 2002, 41–51). The now-abandoned shop was built of huge yellow poplar logs notched with half-dovetails.

GRISTMILLS

Water-powered gristmills served as focal points for the exchange of goods, services, and gossip as well as for processing grain throughout Appalachia and in much of Tennessee as well. Farmers brought grain to be ground and items to trade and/or sell. The gristmill became the predecessor to the country store because it offered mountain folk a place to trade goods, to exchange ideas, to socialize, and to form a sense of community. Sadly, only two log gristmills show up in the data, one in Sevier County and the other in Dekalb. The Dekalb County mill, located on the edge of the Cumberland Plateau, accounts for one log structure out of 16 outbuildings for the entire county, or 6.25 percent of the log barn and outbuilding structures there.

LOG CHURCHES

Rural churches (Map 33) are so abundant in Tennessee that they appear almost at every crossroad. They are more common than country stores because the rural landscape has lost so many gristmills, stores, and rural post offices. Rural churches don't seem to decline. Most survive, and in some places rural churches grow externally, with splinter groups forming new, small congregations. Everywhere I turn I see white-painted wooden church buildings but very few log churches. In the survey, there are just 12 such buildings: 1 each in Clay, Dekalb, Giles, Hawkins, Knox, Maury, Morgan, and Sevier counties, and 2 each in Hamblen

A dilapidated log church was one of only 18 log buildings in the 1980 survey of Morgan County on the Cumberland Plateau. When the author arrived in 2005, the place was gone. (Courtesy of the Tennessee Historical Commission.)

The Old Union United Methodist Church, established in 1834 in Hawkins County, is a testament to historic preservation. The original log unit measures 30 feet by 27 feet and was built with V-notched oak logs.

The old log portion of the Okolona Church (Overton County) was built in 1890 with half-dovetail notches on oak logs.

and Overton counties. The church in Morgan County is now gone. In Hawkins County, an interesting log church, the Old Union United Methodist Church established in 1834, has a somewhat newer brick sanctuary attached to it. The old log part, built in 1834, measures 30 feet by 27 feet and has V-notched oak logs.

In Overton County, on the Highland Rim area just west of the Cumberland Plateau, is the well-preserved Okolona log church, built in 1890 of oak logs with half-dovetail notches. During its early history, three different congregations held services at this church on alternating Sundays. It had been also used as a school building. Adjacent to it is the newer, white-framed church where most services are now conducted. Special services are still held in the old log building each July (Rehder 2004, 144).

On May 16, 2005, I was working the Eastern Highland Rim area of Overton County. I had just revisited the old log Okolona Church south of Livingstone and was busy field-checking an area west of Livingston. Taking Upper Hilham Road, I sadly worked derelict houses and sought missing structures along the way. Eventually, I came to a stop sign in a shady intersection where, across the road, sat a little log church with a sign proclaiming, "Old Union Meeting House." It featured nice half-dovetail notches cut into huge yellow poplar logs. The building resembled a saddlebag house with two pens and a central chimney. It measured 35 feet 9 inches by 25 feet 11 inches, and the logs were between 11 inches and 18 inches thick. How did I miss the data from the Tennessee Historical Commission's surveys? The book *Upper Cumberland Historic Architecture* came to the rescue with additional information. The Old Union Church at Hilham was built about 1880 by three local craftsmen: Eb Wright, Dillard Eldridge Wright, and John Horner (Dickinson, Birdwell, and Kemp 2002, 19).

LOG SCHOOLS

Just seven log schools (Map 34) appear in my survey data. An additional, restored school in Henderson County was brought to my attention recently. There are two in Blount County, one of which is a replica. Sevier, Hawkins, Macon, Morgan, and Union counties each have one such building. The geographic distribution says little to us other than that we have five in East Tennessee, one on the Cumberland Plateau, one on the northern Highland Rim, and the added one in West Tennessee. In 2005, I discovered that the ones in Macon and Morgan counties were already gone. You might expect log schools to be in some museum setting, and you would be correct. In Blount County, the 1882 Little Greenbrier School near Metcalf Bottoms is protected within the Great Smoky Mountains National Park. Also, the restored Sam Houston Schoolhouse, a state museum site, is located northeast of Maryville.

The Old Union Meeting House (c. 1880) in Overton County measures 35 feet 9 inches (east) by 25 feet 11 inches (north) by 35 feet 8.5 inches (west) by 25 feet 9.5 inches (south). The place was built with half-dovetail notches on yellow poplar logs.

The log school in Union County is a restored log building moved in 1979 from Sharp's Ridge to a site beside the Roy Acuff Museum in Maynardville. The square building measures 20 feet 2 inches by 20 feet 4 inches, with mixed timber of yellow poplar, oak, and pine featuring half-dovetail notches. I am glad that the restoration work done in 2005 used the more traditional yellow poplar logs (Rehder 2006).

A favorite log schoolhouse of mine is the Stone Mountain School, built in 1940 in East Tennessee's Hawkins County. Now converted into a residence, the place appears to be well protected. Located off TN 66 northwest of Rogersville, the log school building is found in Poor Valley, a once appropriately named place that has seen marked improvement. This building is fascinating because it represents one of the last periods of historic log construction in Tennessee, especially for schools. The log treatments are like those of Depression-era log houses, featuring round pine logs with saddle notches. Unlike the other examples, which

Log Barns and Outbuildings

The Stone Mountain School (Poor Valley, Hawkins County) was built in 1940 with saddle notches on round pine logs. The well-preserved building is now a private residence.

are one-room school buildings, this one has several classrooms. It is a huge, H-shaped building with wings on the east and west elevations and a large section in the center.

The West Tennessee example is called the Doe Creek School. Located near Scotts Hill on the eastern border separating Henderson and Decatur counties, the one-room log structure was originally built in 1869–70 and used as a school for eight grades, taught by one teacher, until the early 1950s. It is now a community center and historic site. The little place has been carefully restored with yellow-poplar timbers and half-dovetail notches. I am glad that the preservationist's efforts were so faithful to the original methods, tree species, notches, and dimensions.

Chapter 5

Exceptional Log Places

Having observed thousands of folk structures through the years, I thought it would be intriguing to take a closer look at four sites that represent varying degrees of fragility. The first two sites have escaped from the brink of extinction, their preservation exemplifying what communities and individuals can do to save fragile landscape features. The third site is outright unusual: well protected and preserved by owner-families and the Tennessee Historical Commission, it has suffered unfathomable damage that came not from human hands but from a tornado. The fourth and youngest site is the most vulnerable, the potential victim of a large, upscale, residential mountain resort development. While each place undoubtedly has a deeper human history than I can provide, I hope that they will afford a unique glimpse of our state's heritage as reflected in Tennessee's log buildings.

THE HOUSE THAT MOVED: WALKER SPRINGS (1826–27)

It was a small farmhouse on Fox-Lonas Road in west Knox County, and for more than 20 years my family and I drove by it almost daily. The house might be labeled a formative I-house because it was not quite a full-sized I-house, but it was larger than a regular double-pen Cumberland type. The pen on the west elevation was nearly two stories tall, but the east elevation's pen was just one story high. It resembled those split-level ranchers like the one we once lived in, a home built in 1964 and located in a subdivision about a mile away. Although the old house had sawn, lumber clapboards for weatherboarding, I had always thought of it as a log house. As interesting as it was, the place was so familiar to me that I didn't take any time to analyze or even photograph it. Some time in 1988 the house was demolished. I briefly lamented its demise but chalked up the loss to progress. I was too busy working in remote areas to be bothered by some old house just down the road. For shame! The surrounding developed area was closing in fast around this holdout dairy farm. Subdivisions, a huge apartment complex called Sunchase, a convenience store across the street, and a tennis sports complex to the north and east were just a few of the landscape invaders.

Between 1967 and 1984, Crockett Dyer and his wife Cautella occupied the old house. They were dairy farmers, hard working on that holdout land already surrounded by a suburbanized landscape of schools, houses, condos, churches, and convenience stores. From what I can discern, Dyer had been working the farm for decades. Business directories listed the place with different addresses. Between 1965 and 1975 the address was listed as Rural Route 25, but after 1975 the address became 9241 Fox Lonas Road. The city business directory recorded Crockett Dyer living on the farm from at least 1965 (data for the county did not appear in the city directory before that year) until 1984 when Dyer retired at age 75 and moved off the property. On May 6, 1999, Dyer died at the age of 90; his wife Cautella Dyer died on January 30, 2002 (City Directory Company of Knoxville 1971, 236; annually from 1971 to 1985; City Publishing Company 1965, 108).

After Dyer vacated the house in 1984, the house and farm had various renters. Among them was a business called Cedar Bluff Stables that took over the

In 1984, the "Walker Springs" place was a weather-boarded Cumberland double-pen house. The home, then occupied, was located on Fox Lonas Road in west Knox County. (Courtesy of the Tennessee Historical Commission.)

old dairy barn. In 1988, when the house was torn down, the logs were numbered during the process. These and other parts of the structure were transported by high school students to Marble Springs in south Knox County, a protected state historic site also known as the Governor John Sevier Plantation. It is located on TN 168 (the John Sevier Highway) between Chapman Highway (US 441) and Alcoa Highway (US 129).

Marble Springs was once a home of Gov. John Sevier, a pioneer folk hero and Tennessee's first governor. He served a total of 11 years, from 1796 to 1801 and again from 1803 to 1809 (Bergeron, Ash, and Keith 1999, 70). Sevier set up the Marble Springs farm and occupied it periodically between 1792 and 1815 (West 1995, 71–72). A single-pen cabin, restored with added pine logs, connected by a dogtrot opening to the kitchen, is located on what is believed to be the original house site. University of Tennessee archaeologist Charles Faulkner had teams of students working under and around the Sevier house site for several field seasons. In 2006, a dendrochronology survey was set up for the house. The dendrochronology tree-ring analysis conducted by Henri Grissino-Mayer and Saskia van

In 1988, the Walker Springs structure was moved 18 miles from its west Knox County site to the Marble Springs John Sevier historic site in south Knox County. Only the larger pen, the west elevation on the original, was reconstructed there.

Exceptional Log Places

der Gevel determined the date of 1834–35 for the oldest oak logs in the single-pen structure. No other logs in the structure predated this figure (Grissino-Mayer and van der Gevel 2007).

In 1988, the logs from the old house from Fox Lonas were re-erected into a tall but single-unit structure located about 30 yards west of the Sevier house at the Marble Springs complex. Here the restored building is called the "Walker Springs" place, so named for the general area in west Knoxville where the structure originated. Incidentally, the site called Walker Springs is at least two miles east of the original house site. I would prefer to call it by another name, perhaps after the original owner or a subsequent early owner. We shouldn't call it Fox or Lonas as they were the names of adjacent farms owned by early farmers who lived west and east of the old original farm site in west Knox County.

Marble Springs Plantation in south Knox County was a home of Gov. John Sevier between 1792 and 1815. Dr. Charles Faulkner of the University of Tennessee conducted archeological investigations on the historic site.

Some people believed the structure to have been an inn or tavern and so designated it for the Marble Springs complex. I doubt that the house was big enough to have been an inn. It might have been a tavern, but that also seems unlikely, given the history of the place as a residence on a dairy farm. Its location on a side road called Fox Lonas, off Cedar Bluff Road, and nearly two miles from the main thoroughfare called Kingston Pike suggests that it was probably never an inn or tavern (that is, if one assumes that today's Kingston Pike retains its historic position). The lane now called Fox Lonas Road once connected to Dutchtown Road, which runs through an old German-settled valley west of Cedar Bluff. If this had been the main road in the early nineteenth century, then the place might have served as a tavern. Still, I believe that both the popular name and function of the place are questionable.

The now-restored log building at Marble Springs is almost two stories tall. There are 13 logs per elevation, counting from the foundation sill logs to the topmost logs at the eaves. Mortised loft joists mark the approximate halfway point at log number 8 from the bottom sill on the north elevation. Thus, it is one story and three quarters in actual form. Outside horizontal dimensions are 23 feet 1 inch on both the north and south elevations. The west elevation measures 20 feet 2.5 inches. The east elevation, the gable end with a chimney, measures 19 feet 7.5 inches. The structure's logs are oak and measure 9 inches in average thickness. The chinking is modern tinted cement. A single chimney 7 feet wide and made of rough-cut limestone secures the east elevation. The entrance on the north elevation features a single door (3 feet 6 inches) offset to the left of center and two windows set equally but far apart. The upper level has two small half-windows set closer together on the façade. Compare these placements with the black-and-white photograph taken in 1984. There is a small window behind the chimney on the east elevation and a single door on the west elevation. The south elevation has two doors but only the center one (3 feet 7 inches) is operable. The other unused door is boarded up and was likely an interior doorway in the original structure that stood in west Knox County.

Using dendrochronology techniques in October 2006, Henri Grissino-Mayer, Saskia van der Gevel, Jessica Brogdon, Lisa LaForest, and Philip White prepared numerous tree-ring cores of selected logs on the structure. (Coring logs requires powerful electric drills with tubular bits. After scientists extract linear cores from logs, they fill the holes with cork plugs that match the diameter and length of the tree-ring core.) After months of precise measurements and statistical analysis back in the laboratory, the core's tree rings revealed that logs in the building date to 1826–27 (Grissino-Meyer and van der Gevel 2007). Dates merely tell us when the trees were cut. Cut dates usually coincide with construction dates within a range of days to months but rarely years. From these dates we can assume that the original house could have been built as early as 1826.

SADDLEBAG: THE HAMILTON-TOLLIVER PLACE (PRE-1829)

Thirty miles north of Knoxville, in Union County northeast of Maynardville, is a log saddlebag house. I first encountered it in 1968. One of my first graduate students, Jim O'Malley, had been exploring East Tennessee for I-houses while researching his thesis and discovered this simple little two-pen saddlebag. It was not an I-house, never had been, but Jim thought it was special enough to drag me out into the field to look at it. The intriguing house had exposed oak logs with neat half-dovetail notches. The stone and mud chinking between the logs, the crumbling central chimney, and rusting tin roof gave it charm as well as a sense of history. Both of us were "not from around here" and new to the area. So, the house became a talisman, a symbol of pioneer folk life that we did not expect to witness too often again anywhere else. In this kind of exploratory fieldwork, every discovery is unique, exciting, and seems important at the time. The house stood out because it was the first really good example of a log saddlebag that either of us had seen in the field at any time, anywhere. It remains the best. For decades, I have made unique discoveries in inventory fieldwork, such as the surveys conducted for the Tennessee Historical Commission. But somehow, even after all of that, this little house has remained particularly special.

Since 1968, the saddlebag has had a rebricked chimney and a new roof put on it, features we observed when we surveyed it in 1979 for the Tennessee Historical Commission. Aside from a few cosmetic modifications and repairs done to the porches, the house retains its original overall dimensions: 18 feet 10 inches deep by 45 feet 8 inches wide. Each pen is different and was built at a different time. The older east elevation pen was built sometime prior to 1829 and measures 21 feet 10 inches wide by 18 feet 10 inches deep. This older pen is also taller with a story-and-a-half height. The slightly smaller west-elevation pen has dimensions of 18 feet by 19 feet and was built only a few years afterwards, or so I believe. The chimney space between the pens (see photo, p. 118) is 4 feet 10 inches wide. The porches add another 9 feet 2 inches to the front and 9 feet 9 inches to the back of the structure. The floor plan remains a simple one with the two pens separated by the central chimney.

Built at some time before 1829, this saddlebag log house remains a remarkably well-preserved example of Tennessee's pioneer past (Bullen 2006).

TENNESSEE'S LARGEST HISTORIC LOG BUILDING: WYNNEWOOD (1828)

Wynnewood is an enormous place in Sumner County, Tennessee. Some say it is the largest standing log building in the state, or perhaps even the country. It is

This little saddlebag house has been a favorite of the author's since 1968. The Hamilton-Tolliver place was built sometime prior to 1829 in Union County.

certainly the largest log building I have ever seen, and I have seen thousands of log structures here and abroad. Wynnewood's main structure is 110 feet long and 21 feet wide under one roof. With the kitchen, a detached log unit connected by a breezeway, the structure lengthens to 142 feet. The site was first named "Wynnewood" in 1940.

When I first wrote those words to describe Wynnewood on a sparkling sunny day in May 2005, I thought that nothing could ever do damage to such a magnificent structure. I was wrong. On the night of February 6, 2008, a powerful tornado, one of an outbreak that slashed across Tennessee, ripped and destroyed the roof and upper floor of Wynnewood (Rogers 2008). Sadly, nearly two dozen Tennesseans lost their lives on that fateful night of storms.

Wynnewood was originally built as a stagecoach inn and resort spa hotel in 1828. The site is located at Castalian Springs, earlier known as Bledsoe's Lick, on Tennessee Highway 25, seven miles east of Gallatin in Sumner County, and about 34 miles northeast of Nashville. The most thorough historical information on Wynnewood comes from a four-part series of articles written by Walter Durham

Details of the central chimney in the Hamilton-Tolliver place indicate that limestone was the original construction material before the chimney was later rebuilt with bricks. The chimney area was a storage place, and in some saddlebags, the warm sheltered space made for a convenient chicken coop.

for the *Tennessee Historical Quarterly* (Durham 1974a, 127–56; 1974b; 297–321; 1974c; 389–409; and 1974d, 32–47; see also West 1995, 315). Thankfully, Durham gathered the articles together into a tidy book titled *Wynnewood: Bledsoe's Castalian Springs, Tennessee*, published in 1994.

The two-story structure combines a huge dogtrot part and a saddlebag part. The overall dimensions are 110 by 21 feet with 10 rooms under one roof. Please don't call the building a dogtrot or a saddlebag, however, even though it may contain elements of both. We cannot call it an I-house either because it is too wide. In general plan, Wynnewood is two stories tall by one room deep by five rooms long.

There are five rooms on each floor. From east to west, the first-floor plan is a 2–1–2-room layout while the second-floor plan is a 1–1–1–2-room layout. The north elevation reveals the dogtrot and saddlebag portions best, with the dogtrot part nearer the east elevation and the saddlebag part to the west. Architectural elements on the north elevation from east to west include:

(1) an outside limestone chimney;
(2) the large east section of the dogtrot, with six windows (three on the first floor, which has two rooms, and three on the second floor, which has one large room that was originally a bunkroom for male guests and later served as a civic-club meeting room);

(3) the open dogtrot passage, which is 18 feet 1 inch wide by 21 feet long, and has front steps and a porch on the first floor and is enclosed on the second floor but lit by two windows;
(4) the west part of the dogtrot portion, which should also be recognized as the east portion of the saddlebag, with four windows (two up and two down);
(5) the central chimney for the saddlebag, which is enclosed but has a small window on the first floor;

Wynnewood's north elevation and west gable end indicate the impressive size of the structure, which was first built as a stagecoach inn and subsequently became a residence, a nineteenth-century spa, a residence again, and, since 1971, a historic site.

A 2008 tornado did terrible damage to Wynnewood, especially its upper floor. (Courtesy of the Tennessee Historical Commission.)

Exceptional Log Places

(6) the west portion of the saddlebag section, with six windows (three up and three down) unevenly set but marking two rooms on each floor; and

(7) the west elevation's large limestone chimney.

There are 14 logs from the ground-level sill log to the topmost log at the eaves. Mortised loft joists are fitted into log number 8 to create the ceiling for the first floor; these in turn become the floor joists for the second-floor level. At the eaves are additional loft joists, rafters, and other roof features. The original roof was made with cedar shakes. A composite roof was put on the structure in the 1950s (Durham 1974a, 127; Durham 1994, 9). In recent years, all roofing has returned to genuine cedar shakes.

Outside stairs and an entrance lead through and into the dogtrot passage. Stairs in the open dogtrot proper lead to rooms on the second floor on the east

In plan, Wynnewood's north elevation (front) at left has an open dogtrot breezeway. On the right, the structure shows saddlebag tendencies with a central chimney. These are loose labelings, however; Wynnewood, in fact, is a unique, indeed extraordinary log building.

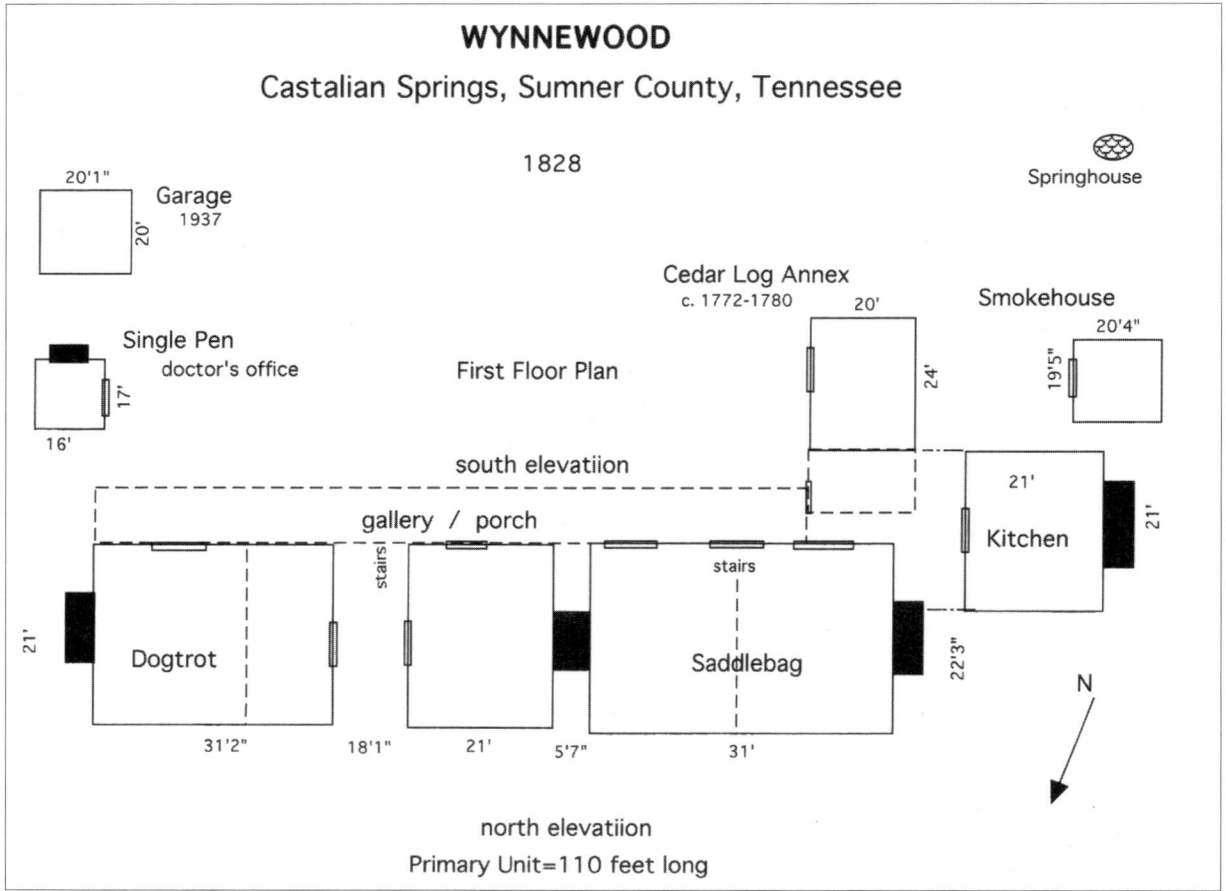

end. A second set of stairs on the west end (one room in from the west elevation) lead internally to the second floor. On the south elevation, doors for first-floor rooms open onto a porch or gallery. The south elevation's gallery extends 110 feet along the long axis of the main structure. In 1899, the gallery's overhang was lowered from just under the eaves to its present position halfway down so that it only shades the first floor. Windows on the south elevation match the patterns of those on the north elevation.

Each east and west elevation has a large limestone chimney that measures 7 feet wide. On the west elevation is a one-story log kitchen that measures a tidy 21 feet by 21 feet. This large detached appendage has an exceptionally massive 11-foot-wide limestone chimney on the west elevation. A covered passage separates the kitchen from the main house. In much of the South, it was customary to separate kitchen from house because of the fire danger and to keep kitchen heat from entering the house. The kitchen has access to a cellar that affords cool storage conditions.

South of the kitchen is another extremely old log building. This two-story annex measures 20 by 24 feet and is constructed with cedar logs. No other log structure at Wynnewood contains cedar, and it is believed that this log house possibly predates the inn and could have been built by the initial settler, Isaac Bledsoe, perhaps in the 1772–80 period. This log structure was connected by a board-and-batten covered passageway to the main house in 1899. It once had a stone fireplace and chimney, but these are now gone. Described as part of General James Winchester's estate in 1829, this may have been the "comfortable cabin" or "workshop" of the two log buildings in an early property description (Durham 1974a, 138; Durham 1994, 10).

Wynnewood's smokehouse (19 feet 5 inches by 20 feet 4 inches) is located just west and south of the log annex and only a few feet from the southwest corner of the kitchen.

To the southeast of the inn, about 40 feet away, is another log house, a single-pen with large limestone chimney. Its dimensions are 16 by 17 feet, and the chimney is almost 6 feet wide. Oriented with its door to the west and gables forming north and south elevations, the pen appears to have been built at about the same time as the inn. Over the years it has seen many different functions: summer cottage, doctor's office and quarters, bachelor's quarters, and school (Durham 1974a, 138; Durham 1994, 10). Currently it is displayed as a doctor's office with medical artifacts.

In 1899, the site, under the name "Castalian Springs Hotel," became a genuine resort spa. Two rows of cottages, each containing 10 one-room board-and-batten cabins were built in the back of the property about 100 feet behind the log inn. The nineteenth-century resort also sported a bowing alley, dance pavilion,

The south elevation of Wynnewood's main house has entry doors and a covered porch. The cedar log structure (left) is thought to be an original pen that is older than Wynnewood itself.

poolroom, and a large dining room (Durham 1974b, 315–16; Durham 1994, 50). Only one cottage remains today.

Wynnewood's interiors for all five of the first-floor rooms remained unfinished until 1836. At that time, Almira Wynne arranged to have them plastered according to instructions sent by her husband, Alfred Wynne, who was in Natchez, Mississippi, conducting business, most likely selling slaves. The western rooms on the second floor were plastered sometime later. Fortunately for the architectural observer, the large bunkhouse/meeting room on the east end's second floor was kept in its original form with exposed logs to the interior (Durham 1974a, 137; Durham 1994, 9).

Timbers for the logs in Wynnewood are mostly oak with some walnut and ash as well. The builders used only V notches, an indication of both age and craftsmanship. The smokehouse is almost entirely built of black walnut. The log annex is entirely cedar. Some logs in the main structure are huge, with single lengths of 32 feet. Most logs measure 16 inches wide by 8 inches thick. They are extremely heavy, to be sure. In my office at the University of Tennessee, I have a V-notched oak log that measures only 3 feet long, 10 inches wide, and 8 inches

The logs at Wynnewood consist mostly of V-notched oak and black walnut logs.

thick; but it weighs 60 pounds. Imagine the weight of Wynnewood's logs, which are 10 times longer and much wider.

Three partners—Alfred Royal Wynne, Stephen R. Roberts, and William Cage—built Wynnewood in 1828 as a stagecoach inn and mineral springs resort on the main road about 34 miles northeast of Nashville. The nearby mineral spring was then called Bledsoe's Lick. The land had been part of the estate of Gen. James Winchester, whose daughter Almira Winchester Wynne (wife of Alfred Wynne) inherited 312 acres—the spring and the house site that became Wynnewood.

The Winchesters had also been the original owners of the famous limestone mansion called Cragfont built in 1798–1802 and located two miles west of Wynnewood. For more on Cragfont, see the section "Stone Houses in a Land of Logs" in chapter 3. Around 1830, Wynne changed the place name from Bledsoe's Lick to Castalian Springs. It was an unusual name suggested by his wife's brother, Valerius Publicola Winchester, a University of Nashville student, who was reminded of the Castalian Springs in Greek mythology (Durham 1974a, 140; Durham 1994, 11). With a seemingly more attractive name for the spring site, the community around Wynnewood became Castalian Springs and remains so today.

Exceptional Log Places

The stagecoach-inn business failed in 1834, when the main east-west route in the area was moved south 12 miles away to the route now known as US 70, which passes through Lebanon, Tennessee. Alfred Wynne bought out the two other partners and moved his family into the huge structure. The enormous house was obviously needed as the Wynnes had 14 children there between 1825 and 1850. Still, in later years the site continued to be used commercially as a spa resort focused on the springs with additional cabins in back. Alfred Wynne (1800–1893), businessman, slave owner and trader, and land speculator in Tennessee and Texas, lived there until he died in 1893. The property remained in the Wynne family through successive generations until 1971, when George Winchester Wynne, a grandson of the original owner/builder, conveyed the property to the State of Tennessee as a historic site.

Wynnewood serves as a reminder of the capacity and creativity of people at a time when log construction was still mostly focused on single- and double-pen construction and little more. While some I-houses were being built with logs, fewer four pens were being constructed with logs because of the size, weight, and height complexities. To build a structure as large as Wynnewood would require imagination, skill, and enormous labor, whether accomplished in 1828, 1928, or 2008.

Since 2008, in fact, the tornado-damaged Wynnewood and adjacent structures have been largely restored. The place faces a new threat, however. Plans for a nearby rock quarry have sparked fears that the explosive methods used in quarrying could damage the historic structures. Lawsuits to stop development of the quarry have thus been initiated (Bledsoe Lick Historical Association website 2011; Save Castalian Springs! blog 2011).

A TWENTIETH-CENTURY LOG COMPLEX: THE MEEK WILLIAMS PLACE (1902)

In East Tennessee's Sevier County, on the south side of the western part of English Mountain, are the remains of a twentieth-century, folk landscape at the Meek Williams place. The 175-acre farm is no longer occupied, but it has an interesting landscape expression. The one-story, two-pen house is a saddlebag type with a central chimney flanked by pens on either side. The house has a huge chimney made of local sandstone rocks that marks the center of the roof between the two pens. The saddlebag core measures 29 feet 9 inches wide by 15 feet 3 inches deep. The house has a multitude of additions and modifications, but to the trained eye of a vernacular architectural geographer, it is still a basic saddlebag folk house.

This small saddlebag house once housed Meek Williams (1878–1960), his wife, Elsie Williams (1880–1954), and their nine children.

The place has had three additional rooms and two porches added to it. Meek Williams (1878–1960) and his wife Elsie had nine children here, and they needed space to house everyone. One addition is a small bedroom (7 feet 9 inches by 15 feet 3 inches), which forms part of the west elevation. On the north elevation in back is a very small room (5 feet 2 inches wide). Beyond is a large room that dominates the north and east elevations. This space serves as the dining room and kitchen and has porches on three sides—the east, north, and west elevations.

The place has been identified as a log house, but to my eye, it does not appear to be one. Log houses have thick walls, deep windowsills, and deep door thresholds. This place has thin walls. Also, most log saddlebag houses have a chimney space that appears as a gap between the two pens. This house does not. Short of prying weatherboarding away from the frame, I cannot definitely say that internally the place is a log house.

Exceptional Log Places

It is a saddlebag, for sure, but sided with board-and-batten sawn lumber using the familiar pattern of wide and narrow boards set up in a vertical manner and nailed to an internal frame of sawn light wooden studs, sills, and corner posts. I am certain that the rooms added later are of board-and-batten construction as well. Between the 1880s and 1940s, board-and-batten construction was popular in logging and coal camps and on farms that needed buildings constructed of cheap sawmill lumber (Rehder 2004, 321). Here in the mountains, Meek Williams used board-and-batten construction because sawmilled lumber was readily available from trees right there on the farm; plus, it was a simple, popular technique for external weatherboarding, with the battens covering the spaces between boards to keep out cold winds (Rehder 2004, 112–13).

Log outbuildings on the site consist of a two-crib barn, a smokehouse, and a hog pen located just to the west of the house site. The huge barn is located about 30 yards downhill from the smokehouse and to the west of the saddlebag. The barn has three parts, two of which are built of logs. Facing the barn from the more accessible south elevation, the barn's elements are, from east to west: a log corn crib (6 feet 3 inches by 16 feet 9 inches); an open drive-through space (10 feet 6 inches wide); a large log crib (12 feet by 20 feet 1 inch); another open drive-through space (10 feet 10 inches wide); and finally a large frame and weatherboarded barn-and-hayloft element (25 feet 5 inches by 40 feet 5 inches). As of 2006, the barn was still used for storing hay. A detail that might escape

The complex barn on the Meek Williams place includes a log corn crib (right), a large log crib in the center, a framed lumber section (left), and a huge loft above.

the casual observer is the presence of homemade latches on the barn and other outbuildings—another indication of the self-sufficient way of life once required of Appalachian folk.

The smokehouse, now dismantled, lay between the barn and house but nearer the house. The log structure's dimensions (11 feet 4 inches by 15 feet 4 inches and 6 feet tall) were typical of smokehouses in Southern Appalachia. About 30 yards up the hill and across the branch is a low log crib that may have once been used as a hog pen. The small dilapidated building (8 feet by 10 feet) is crudely constructed with small logs, perhaps from some other structure. All of the other outbuildings near this end of the complex were made with sawn lumber, vertically set but not in the familiar board-and-batten technique.

The log buildings feature saddle-V notches on small-diameter pine logs; however, a few logs in the barn are oak. These indicate several important elements in reading the landscape. First, the V parts of the notches are on the upper sides of the logs and inverted. The bottoms of the logs are rounded and thus classified as part of the saddle-notch types; thus combined the notch type here is called saddle-V (Rehder 2004, 78–92). Second, the preponderance of pine trees indicates the mountain ecology of this side of English Mountain, especially on the lower south-facing slopes, which had sunny, warm conditions. It would be unusual to find many tree species other than the dominant pine and a few scattered oaks on this side of the mountain and especially at this late time in the history of log construction. The third observation is that the soft pines historically are the last tree of choice for construction because most species rot so easily. Throughout the region, the first choice has been yellow poplar, followed by oak, and then pine. At the Meek Williams place, however, we did observe some oak logs in the mix of logs in the barn, and thus these may be the oldest logs by species on site.

In other parts of Tennessee, cedar or chestnut, where available, might enter the sequence but usually after oak. Chestnut, the monarch of Appalachian forests, became an unexpected resource for log-house and fence construction in the 1925–38 period when an Asian fungus killed the American chestnut in one of the worst blights to hit U.S. forests. The only problem is that this part of English Mountain doesn't have chestnut trees, and even if it did, it was unlikely that settlers would have destroyed such a valuable nut and bark tree for house and fence construction. It was only after the blight hit that Appalachian people made wholesale construction uses of millions of dead chestnut trees.

The fourth observation is that the buildings here at the Meek Williams Place were built late, around 1902, and for some log outbuildings after 1940. This was a late time for log construction because of the dominance of board-and-batten in the house and its many additions. It would appear that the Williams family

The large center crib in the Meek Williams barn was built with pine and oak logs with saddle-V notches.

spent their time, energy, and resources on the sawmill lumber for the house—an indicator of putting the "best" resources into the dwelling. Then, almost as an afterthought, the smokehouse and barn were fashioned with the small-diameter trees that remained available. I have analyzed aerial photography of the site, and the large barn did not appear until after 1940.

How old are the log structures at the Meek Williams Place? One way of determining that is to analyze the pattern of tree rings through the science of dendrochronology. This method enables the researcher to determine past climatic patterns of wet and dry years based on tree-ring widths. The number and pattern of rings can be correlated to a known chronology of base data for determining the age of the log structures. Dendrochronology can tell us when the trees were cut, though not when log buildings were built.

In early 2006, Chris Underwood, a dendrochronology graduate student in the UT Department of Geography, and I investigated the barn site to determine whether it was feasible to core some of the logs. Unfortunately, the logs were not old enough: they needed to be 50 years old or older when they were cut to be considered valid data in a scientific dendrochronology study. Moreover, we might have gotten better samples if we had had log cross-sections instead of drilled cores. As it turned out, we had neither, so this part of the investigation was closed.

A second way to determine the general age of structures is to investigate the historic pattern of ownership. As far as I can determine, Meek Williams initiated his farm settlement at the site on or before 1902. The family unit of Williams, his wife, Elsie, and their nine children maintained the farm until 2005. Using the limited tree-ring data taken from the largest oaks and going by what I know about the ownership record, I can surmise the following chronology for the log barn. First, the oldest logs in the barn have 47 tree rings on them, meaning that they are 47 years old. Second, from aerial photographic evidence, we know that the barn was built sometime after 1940. Third, we know that Meek Williams bought acreage in 1902. Putting it all together, we can presume that if Meek Williams first settled the site in 1902, then the trees that would later provide the barn's logs were between one and seven years old. Williams would have to wait another 40 years before the trees were of sufficient size for log construction. Imprecise as this is, we at least have an estimate of the barn's initial date: sometime between 1940 and 1949.

As a correlation to our limited dendrochronology, I conducted a deed-records search to determine the historical succession of the Meek Williams place. The succession of ownership is incomplete, but what I do have is interesting. I am uncertain when the place first became the property of Meek Williams (1878–1960).

However, in 1902, Meek Williams at age 24 purchased a 15-acre tract from Henry Webb. Sixteen years later, Williams added another 15-acre tract that he purchased from Elvin Hurst (1850–1935), the man for whom the nearby stream Elvin Branch is named. Earlier, in 1913, Elvin Hurst had acquired this tract from George Hurst but sold it to Meek Williams in 1918. Williams continued to acquire more land by buying 50 acres from Ara T. Weeks in 1921 and 15 more acres from J. C. Hurst in 1927. Not through yet, Williams added 30 more acres in 1938 from Henderson Hurst. And with that, these acquired tracts added up to 125 acres of the 175-acre farm. In August 2005, the property was acquired by Eagle Rock Development LLC, became a part of the Preserve at English Mountain, and ended the current ownership succession (Sevier County, TN, Warranty Deed Book 2319, 161).

The Williams name is an old, established one that dates to settlers in the early nineteenth century: the oldest gravesite nearby is that of Nancy Ann Williams (1782–1866). Meek Williams was born in 1878 and died in 1960. His wife, Elsie, was born in 1880 and died in 1954. Together they had nine children—six boys and three girls. One child, Willard. died in 1922. Eight of the children grew to adulthood, but only two ever married. The eight children lived long lives, many well into their 80s, but all nine children were deceased by 2002. It appears that most of the family members lived in the saddlebag house long after Meek died in 1960. The last resident at the place was Meek's son Larce Wilfred Williams (1920–2002), who died on May 24, 2002. A makeshift handicap ramp built sometime after 1992 was a part of the front of the structure. As of this writing in December 2006, the Meek Williams place, though abandoned, wonderfully reflects an ancient, pioneer, folk way of life that extended into the twentieth century here on English Mountain, Tennessee. Of few places in America can the same be said.

Epilogue

When you travel around Tennessee, be on the lookout for log houses or log barns out on the open landscape. With so many structures now gone, you are more likely to find log buildings preserved in outdoor museums or in state and federal parks. I can suggest several log places that are accessible to the public; some are free and some charge an admission fee.

In East Tennessee, visit the historic territorial capital, Rocky Mount, on US 11E in Sullivan County. The Netherland Inn in Kingsport (also in Sullivan County) has some restored log buildings behind it. The very best collection of authentic log buildings can be found at the Museum of Appalachia just off I-75 (Exit 122) in Anderson County. The Governor John Sevier Plantation at Marble Springs has three log places on John Sevier Pike (TN168) in Knox County; one of them is the "house that moved" described in chapter 5. A recent outdoor-indoor museum is the Great Smoky Mountain Heritage Museum on US 321 in Townsend (Blount County). Not far from Townsend, you can enter the Great Smoky Mountains National Park; at the Y in the road, hang a right and visit Cades Cove to view an impressive number of original and restored log structures along an 11-mile loop. Also in the Great Smoky Mountains National Park, you can examine log buildings at Greenbrier School and the Walker Sisters place near Metcalf Bottoms. In Gatlinburg, turn at traffic light number 8 to enter the GSMNP and visit the Noah "Bud" Ogle place and Roaring Fork Motor Nature Trail. The last blockhouse in Tennessee is Fort Marr on US 411 in Benton (Polk County) adjacent to the old county jail.

In Middle Tennessee, visit Wynnewood, Tennessee's largest log building, on TN 25 in Castalian Springs in Sumner County. Across the highway is Bledsoe's

The Museum of Appalachia near Norris in Anderson County boasts an excellent collection of material folk culture. The snake fences, cantilever barn (center), saw mill, and haystack seen here are but a small part of the museum's dozens of log buildings and thousands of artifacts.

Lick Historic Park, and just two miles west is the huge stone mansion called Cragfont. East of Nashville on US 70, Andrew Jackson's home, the Hermitage, includes an authentic log cabin on site called Alfred's cabin. Southwest of Nashville on US 70S is Belle Meade Plantation, which has a log dogtrot house on site. A reconstructed living-history site is Mansker's Station located on I-65 north of Nashville, just east of Exit 97.

In West Tennessee, you can visit a restored farm setting called "The Homeplace—1850," located just south of the Kentucky state line on the Trace Road in the TVA's Land-between-the-Lakes area of Stewart County.

To be sure, more authentic and restored historic places can be seen, and I wish we could identify them all. Moreover, I wish we could save the ones that are endangered. If you still have an authentic old log building on your property or know of some in your community, you are certainly fortunate. Old log buildings are so scarce that Tennessee's folk landscapes are rapidly becoming endangered. The decline in the numbers of surviving authentic log buildings is alarming. For

The Great Smoky Mountains Heritage Center, featuring several log buildings and an indoor museum, is located on highway US 321 in Townsend (Blount County).

The preservation of log buildings is not an easy task. Thankfully, some folks maintain and restore their log places, as with this example in Knox County. (Courtesy of the Tennessee Historical Commission.)

example, Grainger County lost 58 percent of its pre-1860 log structures between 1978 and 2002—from 38 to 16. Adjacent Union County lost 65 percent of its pre-1860 log buildings between 1979 and 2002—with real numbers declining from 34 to 12 (Reding 2002, 54). The two counties were once reasonably well-preserved living museums but lost buildings over the course of 30 years to neglect and the ravages of weather, to vandalism, and to log collectors who bought up old log structures and rebuilt them into chalets elsewhere (Rehder 2004, 147–48). Grainger and Union counties are not alone and, based on an educated guess, I would think that about half the log buildings that were once surveyed across the state between 1978 and 1993 have vanished. Tennessee's endangered species clearly should include the material folk culture expressed in historic, authentic log buildings.

This has been a long journey, but one that I have wanted to describe to you for quite some time. The data collecting and analysis took decades to do, but I think it was worth it. There are counties for which I wish we had systematic surveys of historic structures; unfortunately, we do not. I am getting too old and too wise to consider surveying any more myself. I receive calls all the time from people who own log buildings. They ask, "Can you fix my place?" "Nope," I have to say. I neither build nor repair them. I just record them on maps and photographs and try to make some sense of the landscape heritage that Tennessee's log buildings represent.

Appendix

Distribution Maps

MAP 1

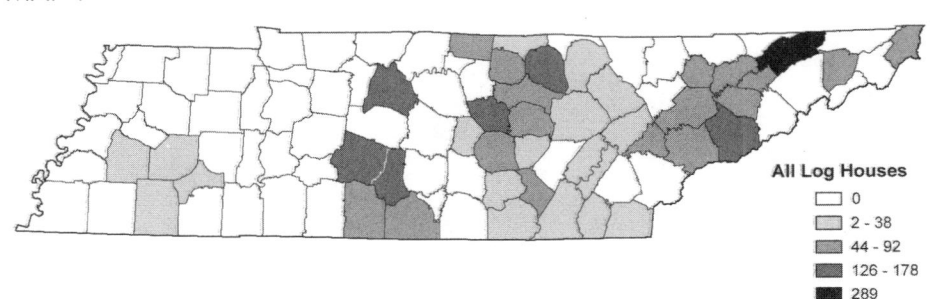

MAP 2

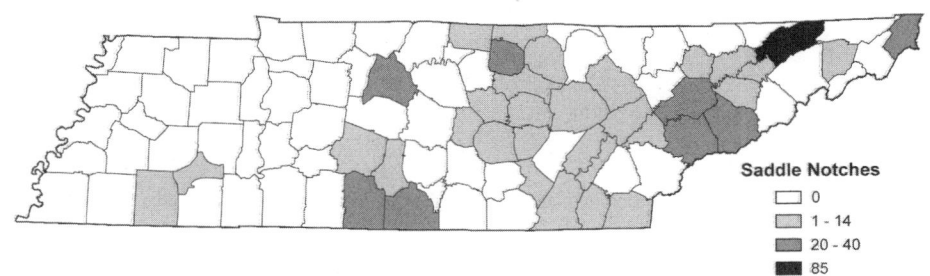

MAP 3

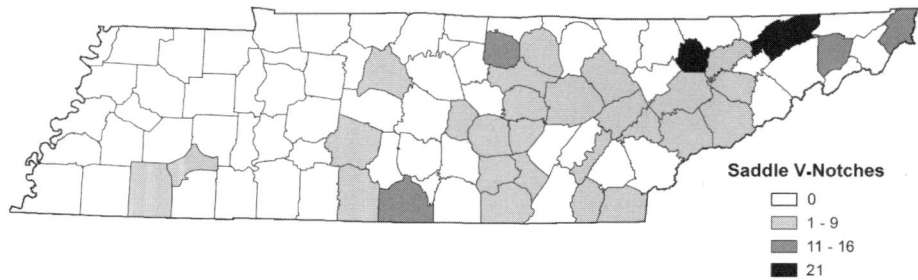

MAP 4

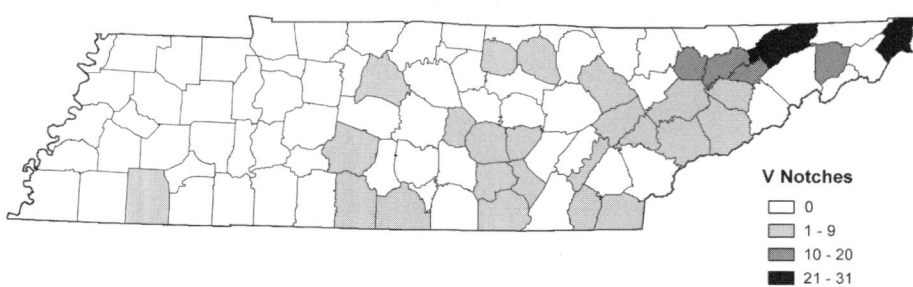

MAP 5

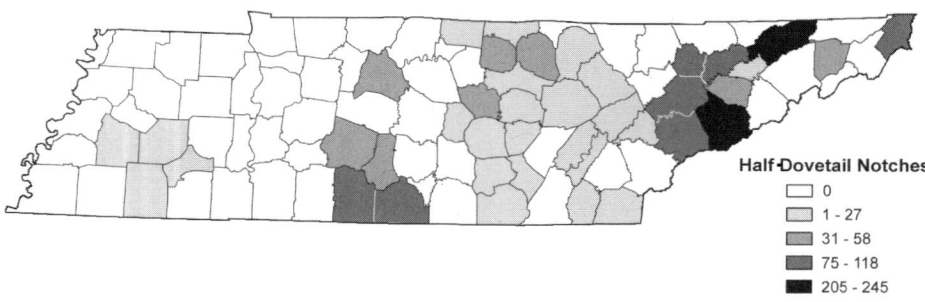

MAP 6

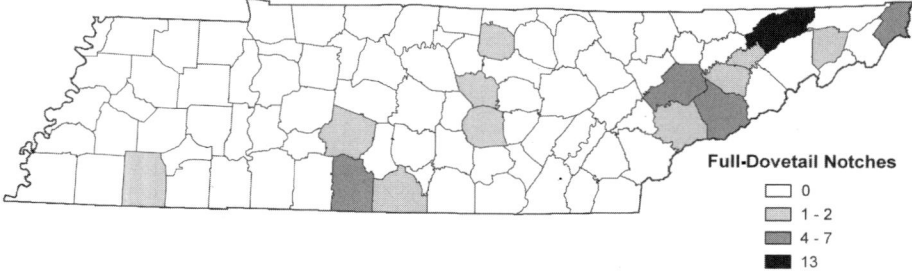

MAP 7

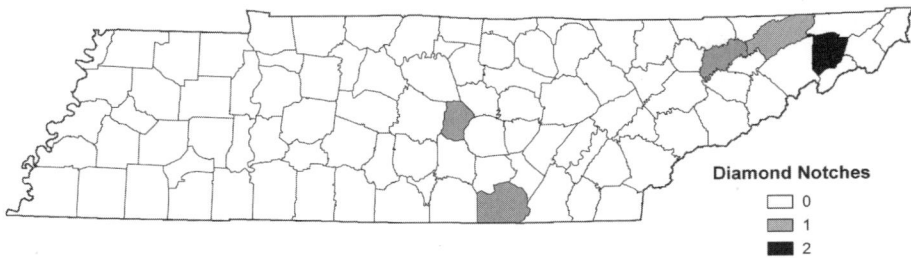

MAP 8

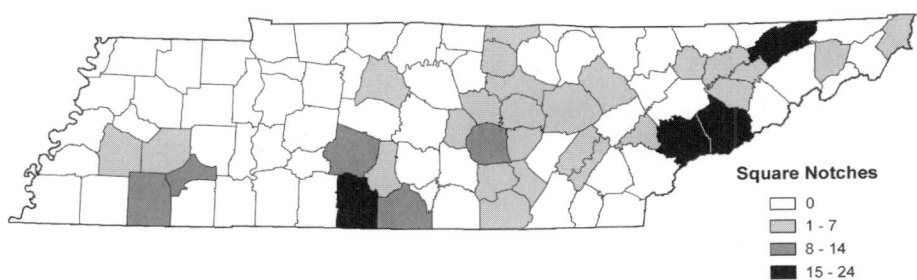

MAP 9

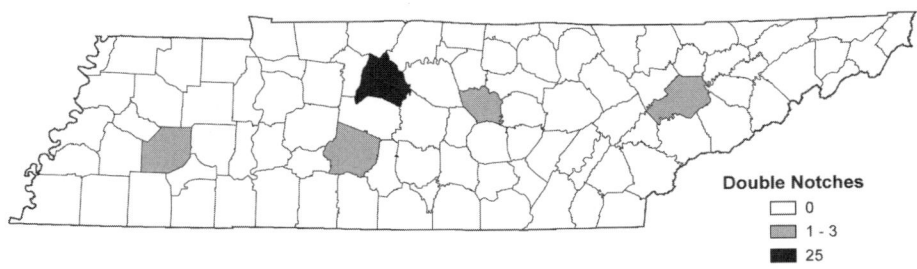

MAP 10

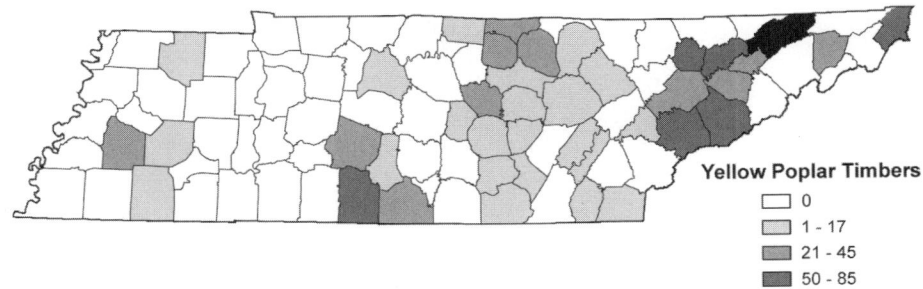

Appendix: Distribution Maps

MAP 11

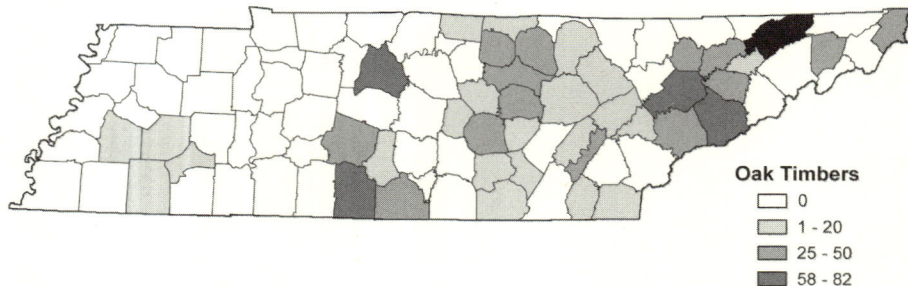

MAP 12

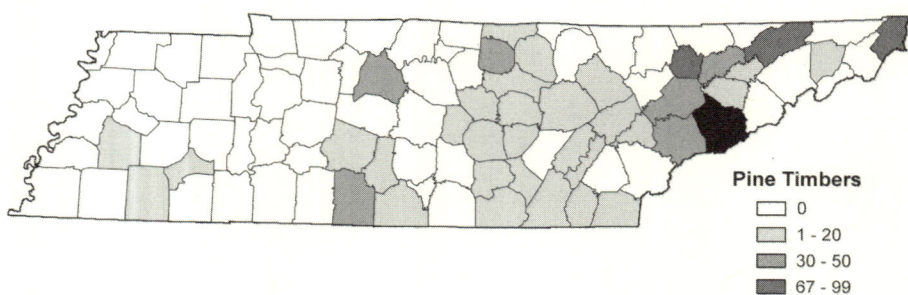

MAP 13

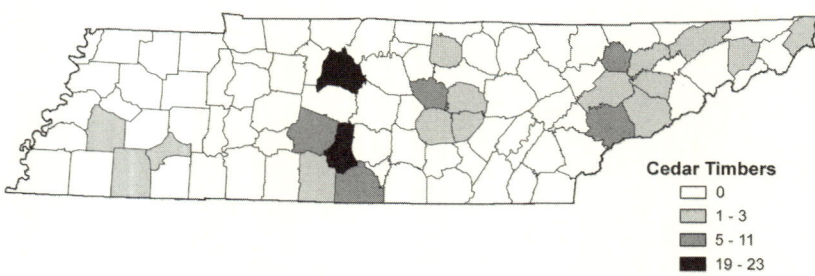

MAP 14

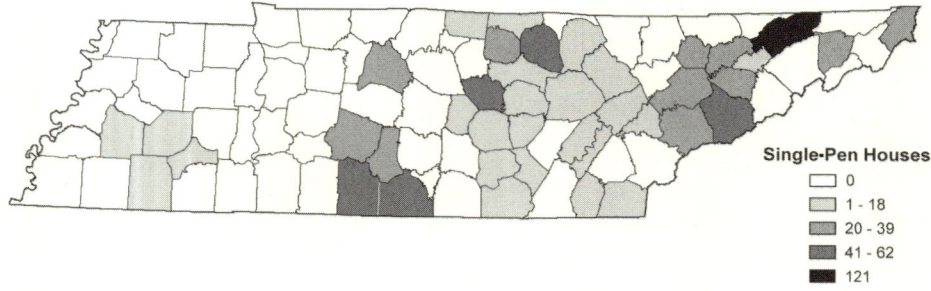

MAP 15

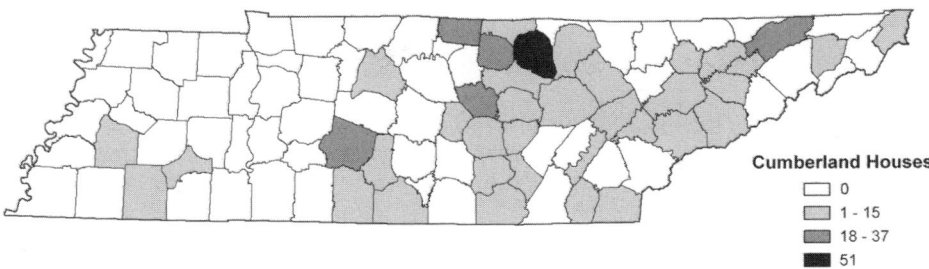

MAP 16

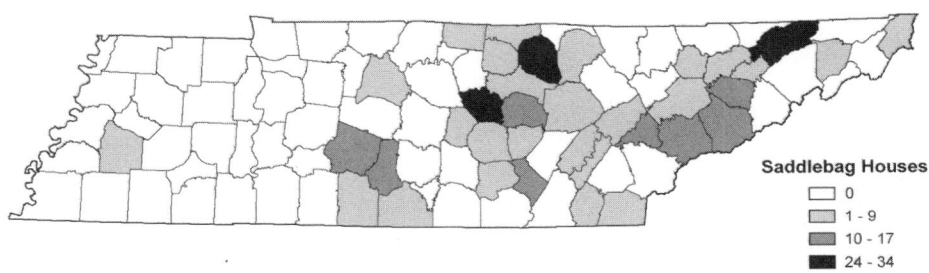

MAP 17

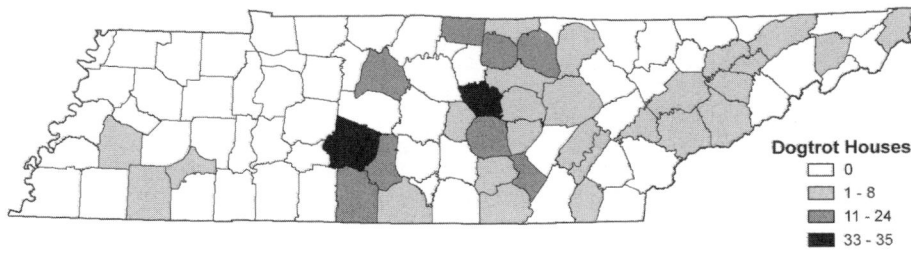

MAP 18

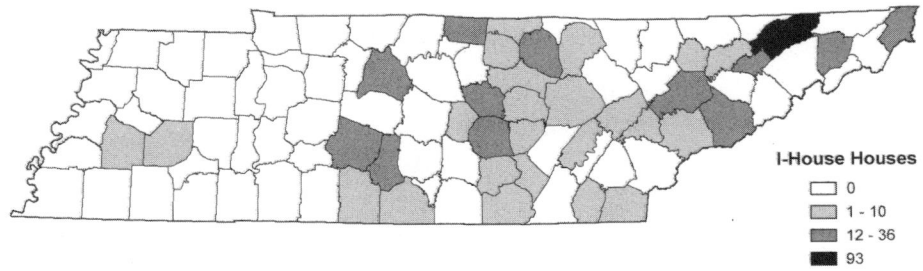

Appendix: Distribution Maps

139

MAP 19

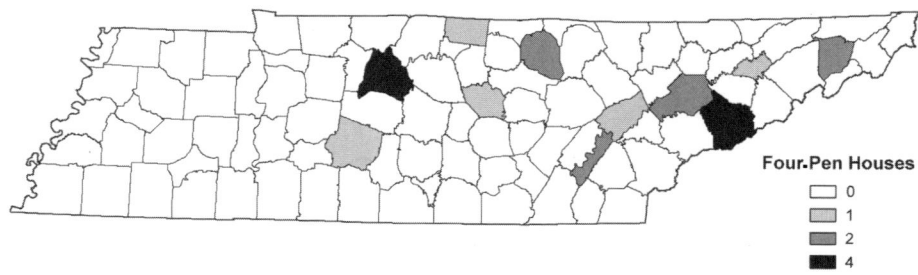

MAP 20

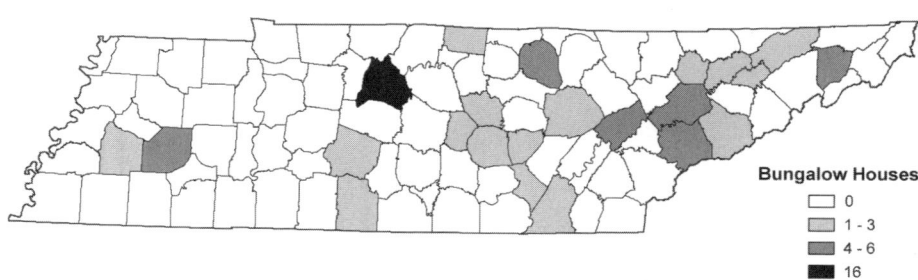

MAP 21

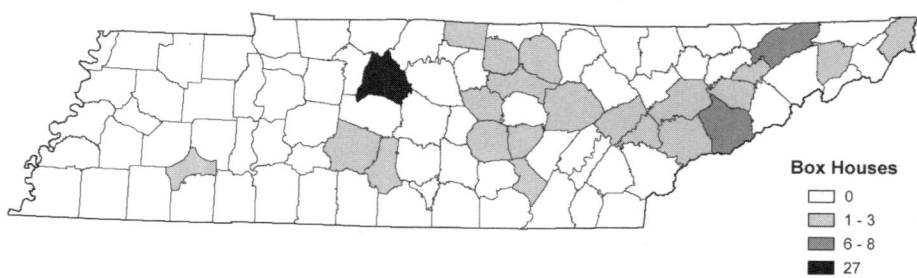

MAP 22

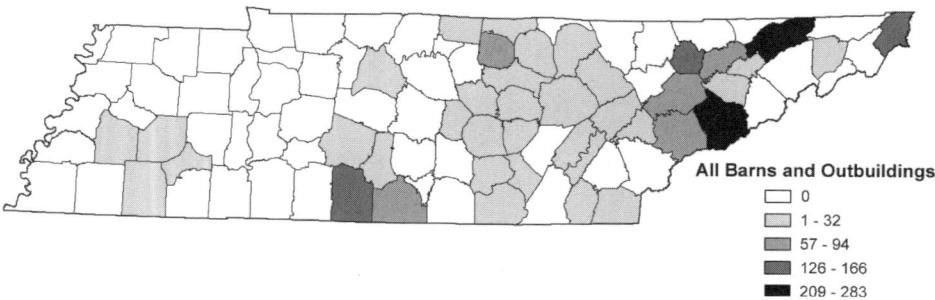

MAP 23

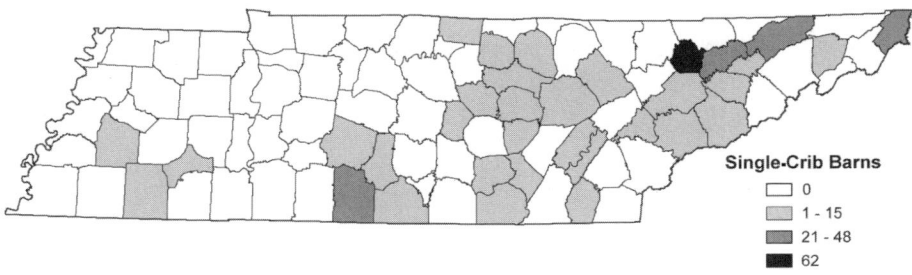

MAP 24

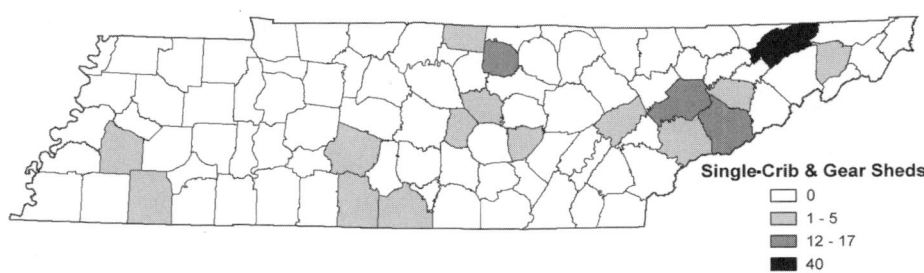

MAP 25

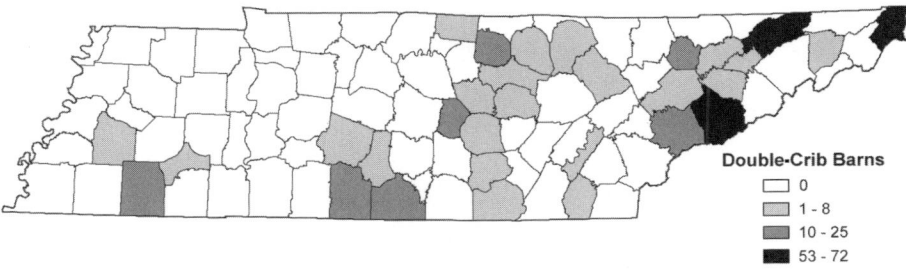

MAP 26

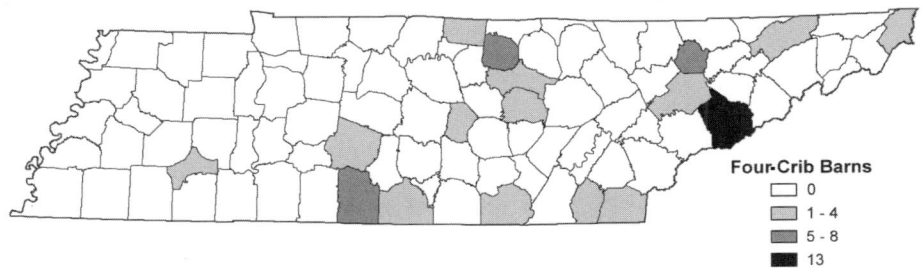

Appendix: Distribution Maps

MAP 27

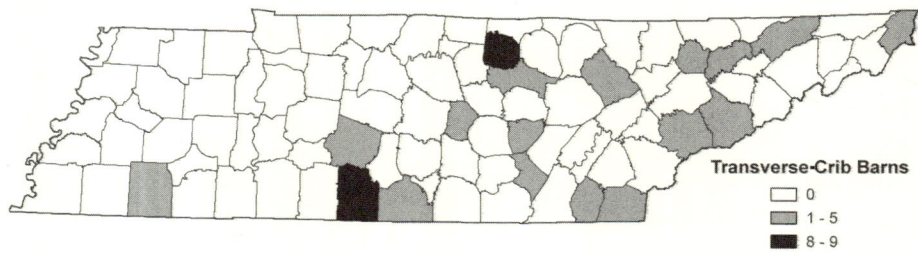

MAP 28

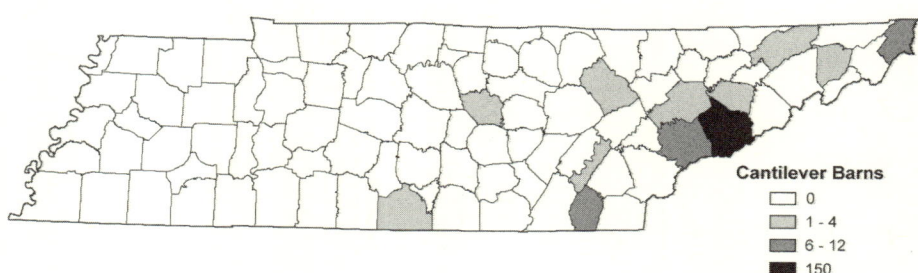

MAP 29

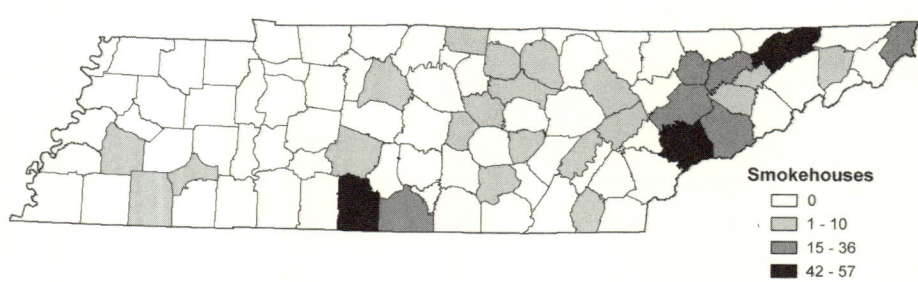

MAP 30

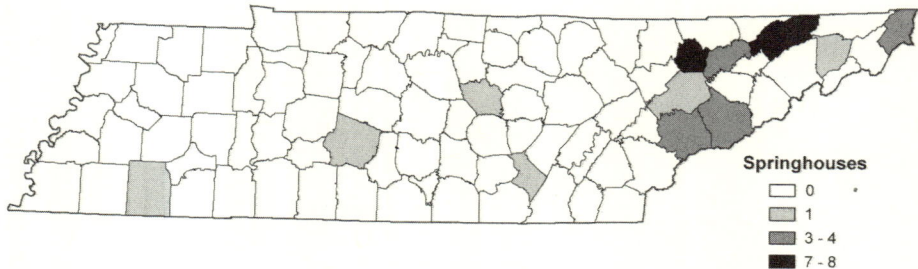

Appendix: Distribution Maps

MAP 31

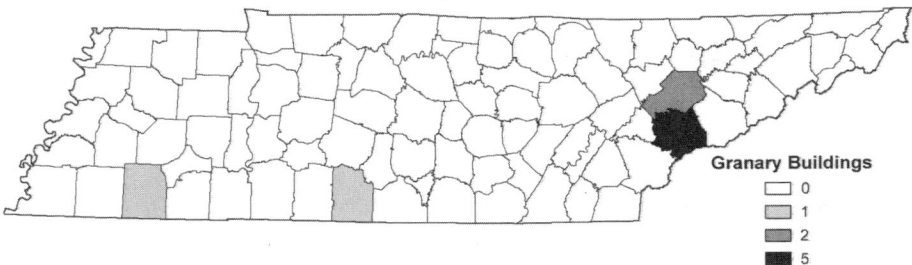

MAP 32

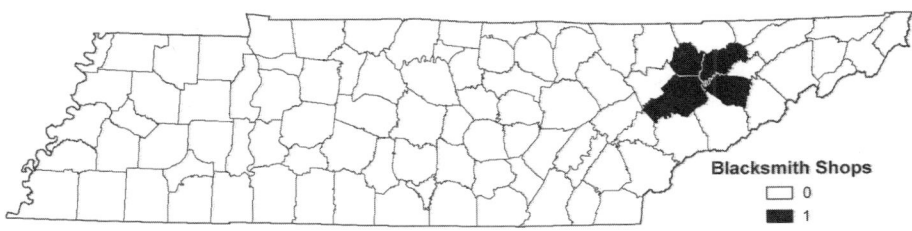

MAP 33

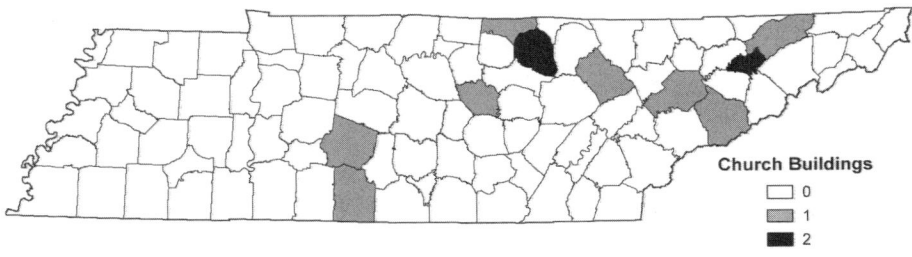

MAP 34

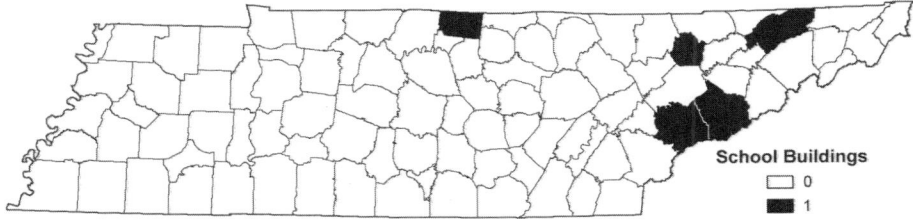

Appendix: Distribution Maps

References

Addy, Sidney O. 1898. *The Evolution of the English House.* London: Swan Sonnenschein.

Alderman, Pat. 1970. *The Overmountain Men.* Johnson City, TN: Overmountain Press.

Ambrosia, Vincent G. 1979. "Log Architecture in Union County, Tennessee: Dwellings, Outbuildings, and Notching Types." Manuscript. Knoxville: Department of Geography, University of Tennessee.

Ball, Donald. 2006. Personal communication. June 11.

Bergeron, Paul H., Stephen Ash, and Jeanette Keith. 1999. *Tennesseans and Their History.* Knoxville: University of Tennessee Press.

Berthoff, Rowland. 1986. "Celtic Mist Over the South." *Journal of Southern History* 52: 523–50.

Bishir, Catherine W. 1990. *North Carolina Architecture.* Chapel Hill: University of North Carolina Press.

Bledsoe's Lick Historical Association website. 2011. "Wynnewood Restoration Project, Tornado Update–2011." http://www.bledsoeslick.com/tornado2011.htm.

Blethen, H. Tyler, and Curtis W. Wood Jr., eds. 2001. *Ulster and North America: Transatlantic Perspectives on the Scotch-Irish.* Tuscaloosa: University of Alabama Press.

Brunskill, R. W. 1978. *Illustrated Handbook of Vernacular Architecture.* London: Faber and Faber.

Bucher, Robert C. 1962. "The Continental Log House." *Pennsylvania Folklife* 12 (4): 14–19.

Bullen, Betty Hamilton. 2006. Personal communication. May 12.

Byrd, William. [1728] 1967. *History of the Dividing Line.* New York: Dover.

Campbell, John C. [1921] 1969. *The Southern Highlander and His Homeland.* Lexington: University of Kentucky Press.

Carlisle, Ronald C. 1982. *An Architectural Study of Some Folk Structures in the Area of the Paintsville Lake Dam Johnson and Morgan Counties, Kentucky.* Report to the U.S. Army Corps of Engineers, Huntington District, Huntington, WV.

Carson, Cary, Joanne Bowen, Willie Graham, Martha McCartney, and Laura Walsh. 2008. "New World, Real World: Improvising English Culture in Seventeenth-Century Virginia." *Journal of Southern History* 74: 31–88.

City Directory Company of Knoxville. 1971–1985. *Knoxville City Directory*. Knoxville: City Directory Company of Knoxville.

City Publishing Company. 1965. *Cross Reference Directory, Greater Knoxville*. Independence, KS: City Publishing Company.

Cooper, Patricia I. 1994. "Cabins and Deerskins: Log Building and the Charles Town Indian Trade." *Tennessee Historical Quarterly* 53 (4): 272–79.

Cox, William E. 1978. *Hensley Settlement: A Mountain Community*. N.p: Eastern National Park and Monument Association.

Davidson, Donald. [1946] 1978. *The Tennessee: The Old River*. Knoxville: University of Tennessee Press.

DeLorme. 2001. *Tennessee Atlas and Gazetteer*. Yarmouth, ME: Delorme.

Dickson, R. J. 1966. *Ulster Emigration to Colonial America, 1718–1775*. London: Routledge and Kegan Paul.-

Dickinson, W. Calvin, Michael E. Birdwell, and Homer D. Kemp. 2002. *Upper Cumberland Historic Architecture*. Franklin, TN: Hillsboro Press.

Dixon, Max. [1976] 1989. *The Wataugans*. Johnson City: Overmountain Press.

Durham, Walter T. 1974a. "Wynnewood." *Tennessee Historical Quarterly* 33: 127–56.

———. 1974b. "Wynnewood, Part II." *Tennessee Historical Quarterly* 33: 297–321.

———. 1974c. "Mexican War Letters to Wynnewood." *Tennessee Historical Quarterly* 33: 389–409.

———. 1974d. "Civil War Letters to Wynnewood." *Tennessee Historical Quarterly* 34: 32–47.

———. 1994. *Wynnewood: Bledsoe's Castalian Springs, Tennessee*. Castalian Springs, TN: Bledsoe's Lick Historical Society.

Dykeman, Wilma. [1955] 1973. *The French Broad*. Knoxville: University of Tennessee Press.

Dykes, Jim. 1968. "Cumberland Plateau's Grassy Cove Is World of Its Own." *Knoxville News-Sentinel*, Nov. 3, D8.

Ensminger, Robert F. 1992. *The Pennsylvania Barn: Its Origin, Evolution, and Distribution in North America*. Baltimore: Johns Hopkins University Press.

Evans, E. Estyn. [1942] 1963. *Irish Heritage: The Landscape, the People, and Their Work*. Dundalk, Ireland: Dundalgan Press.

———. 1974. "Folk Housing in the British Isles in Materials Other than Timber." In *Man and Cultural Heritage: Papers in Honor of Fred B. Kniffen*, ed. H. J. Walker and W. G. Haag, 53–64. Baton Rouge: Louisiana State University School of Geoscience.

Fenneman, Nevin M. 1938. *Physiography of the Eastern United States*. New York: McGraw-Hill.

Ferris, William R., Jr. 1980. "The Dog Trot: A Regional Home and Its Builder." *Perspecta: The Yale Architectural Journal* 17: 68–73.

———. 1986. "The Dogtrot: A Mythic Image in Southern Culture." *Southern Quarterly* 25: 72–85.

Ford, Thomas R., ed. 1967. *The Southern Appalachian Region.* Lexington: University Press of Kentucky.

Fox, Todd. 2001. Unpublished field report and personal communication.

Gavin, Michael. 1979. "The Diamond Notch in Middle Tennessee." *Material Culture* 29 (1): 13–23.

———. 2001. "German American Log Houses of Lawrence County, Tennessee." *Material Culture* 33 (1): 68–83.

———. 2004. "Building with Wood, Brick, and Stone: Vernacular Architecture in Tennessee, 1770–1900." In *A History of Tennessee Arts*, ed. Carroll Van West and Margaret Duncan Binnicker, 17–34. Knoxville: University of Tennessee Press.

Glassie, Henry. 1963. "The Appalachian Log Cabin." *Mountain Life and Work* 39 (4): 5–14.

———. 1964. "The Smaller Outbuildings of the Southern Mountains." *Mountain Life and Work* 40 (1): 21–25.

———. 1968. *Pattern in the Material Folk Culture of the Eastern United States.* Philadelphia: University of Pennsylvania Press.

———. 1975. *Folk Housing in Middle Virginia.* Knoxville: University of Tennessee Press.

———. 1978. "The Types of the Southern Mountain Cabin." In *The Study of American Folklore*, ed. Jan Brunvand, 2nd ed., 390–420. New York: Norton.

Goodspeed, Westin A. [1887] 1972. *Goodspeed's History of Tennessee.* Nashville: Charles and Randy Elder.

Graham, Ian Charles C. 1956. *Colonists from Scotland: Emigration to North America, 1707–1783.* Ithaca, NY: Cornell University Press for American Historical Association.

Graham, Willie, Carter Hudgins, Carl Lounsbury, Fraser Neiman, and James Wittenburg. 2007. "Adaptation and Innovation: Archaeological and Architectural Perspectives on the Seventeenth-Century Chesapeake." *William and Mary Quarterly*, 3rd series, 64: 451–522.

Grissino-Mayer, Henri. 2006–2011. Personal communications.

Grissino-Mayer, Henri D., and Saskia L. van de Gevel. 2007. "Tell-Tale Trees: Historical Dendroarchaeology of Log Structures at Rocky Mount, Piney Flats, Tennessee." *Historical Archaeology* 41 (4): 32–49.

Hankins, Caneta S. 1995. "Hugh Rogan of Counties Donegal and Sumner: Irish Acculturation in Frontier Tennessee." *Tennessee Historical Quarterly* 54: 317.

Hanna, Charles A. [1902] 1968. *The Scotch Irish.* Vols. 1 and 2. Baltimore: Genealogical Publishing Company.

Hofstra, Warren R., and Karl Raitz, eds. 2010. *The Great Valley Road of Virginia: Shenandoah Landscapes from Prehistory to the Present.* Charlottesville: University of Virginia Press.

Hulan, Richard. 1975. "Middle Tennessee and the Dogtrot House." *Pioneer America* 7 (2): 37–47.

Johnson, Hildegard Binder. 1976. *Order Upon the Land.* New York: Oxford University Press.

Jones, Robbie. 1996. *The Historic Architecture of Sevier County, Tennessee.* Sevierville, TN: Smoky Mountain Historical Society.

Jordan, Terry G. 1985. *American Log Buildings: An Old World Heritage.* Chapel Hill: University of North Carolina Press.

Jordan, Terry G., and Matti Kaups. 1989. *The American Backwoods Frontier: An Ethnic and Ecological Interpretation.* Baltimore: Johns Hopkins University Press.

Jordan-Bychkov, Terry G. 1998. "Transverse Crib Barns, the Upland South, and Pennsylvania Extended." *Material Culture* 30 (2): 1–31.

———. 2002. Letter to John B. Rehder. Austin, TX, Dec. 4.

———. 2003. *The Upland South: The Making of an American Folk Region and Landscape.* Santa Fe, NM: Center for American Places.

Kelly, Paul. 1958. *Historic Fort Loudoun.* Vonore, TN: Fort Loudon Association.

Kemmer, John C., III. 2002. Interview. Grassy Cove, TN, June 8.

Kephart, Horace. [1913] 1984. *Our Southern Highlanders.* Knoxville: University of Tennessee Press.

Kilar, Jeremy. W. 1997. "Germans." In *American Immigrant Cultures: Builders of a Nation*, ed. David Levinson and Melvin Ember, 317–22. New York: Simon and Schuster Macmillan.

Kimball, Fiske. [1922] 1966. *Domestic Architecture of the American Colonies and of the Early Republic.* New York: Dover.

King, Duane, Ken Blankenship, and Barbara Duncan. 2006. *Emissaries of Peace: The 1762 Cherokee and British Delegations; Exhibit Catalog.* Cherokee, NC: Museum of the Cherokee Indian.

Kivett, John. 2001. Interview. New Tazewell, TN, Feb. 24.

Kniffen, Fred B. 1936. "Louisiana House Types." *Annals of the Association of American Geographers* 26: 179–93.

———. 1965. "Folk Housing: Key to Diffusion." *Annals of the Association of American Geographers* 55 (4): 549–577.

———. 1969. "On Corner-Timbering." *Pioneer America* 1 (1): 1–8.

———. 1979. "The Geographer's Craft: Why Folk Housing?" *Annals of the Association of American Geographers* 69 (1): 59–63.

Kniffen, Fred B., and Henry Glassie. 1966. "Building in Wood in the Eastern United States: A Time-Place Perspective." *Geographical Review* 56 (1): 40–66.

Layman, Dennis. 2005. Interview. Sevier County, TN, Apr. 14.

Leyburn, James G. 1962. *The Scotch Irish: A Social History.* Chapel Hill: University of North Carolina Press.

Library of Congress. Prints and Photographs Division. Historic American Buildings Surveys (HABS). Washington, DC.

Lounsbury, Carl. 1994. *An Illustrated Glossary of Early Southern Architecture and Landscape.* New York: Oxford University Press.

Lounsbury, Carl. 2010. "Log Building in the Chesapeake." *Vernacular Architecture* 41: 77–82.

Madden, Robert R., and T. Russell Jones. 1977. *Mountain Home: The Walker Family Farmstead, Great Smoky Mountains National Park.* Washington, DC: U.S. Department of the Interior, National Park Service.

Mann, David F. 2002. "The Dendroarchaeology of the Swaggerty Blockhouse, Cocke County, Tennessee." Master's thesis. Department of Geography, University of Tennessee.

Mann, David F., Henri D. Grissino-Mayer, Charles H. Faulkner, and John B. Rehder. 2009. "From Blockhouse to Hog House: The Historical Dendroarchaeology of the

    Swaggerty Blockhouse, Cocke County, Tennessee, U.S.A." *Tree-Ring Research* 65 (1): 57–67.

McIntire, William G. 1958. *Prehistoric Indian Settlements of the Changing Mississippi Delta*. Baton Rouge: Louisiana State University Press.

McNeil, W. K., ed. 1995. *Appalachian Images in Folk and Popular Culture*. 2nd ed. Knoxville: University of Tennessee Press.

McWhiney, Grady. 1988. *Cracker Culture: Celtic Ways in the Old South*. Tuscaloosa: University of Alabama Press.

Mercer, Henry C. 1926. "The Origin of Log Houses in the United States." *Papers, Bucks County Historical Society* 5: 568–83.

Mielnik, Tara Mitchell. "Blount Mansion." In *The Tennessee Encyclopedia of History and Culture*, ed. Carroll Van West, 74. Nashville: Tennessee Historical Society and Rutledge Hill Press.

Moffett, Marian, and Lawrence Wodehouse. 1993. *East Tennessee Cantilever Barns*. Knoxville: University of Tennessee Press.

Montell, William Lynwood, and Michael Lynn Morse. 1976. *Kentucky Folk Architecture*. Lexington: University Press of Kentucky.

Montell, William Lynwood. 1993. *Upper Cumberland Country*. Jackson: University Press of Mississippi.

Moore, Harry L. 1994. *A Geologic Trip across Tennessee by Interstate 40*. Knoxville: University of Tennessee Press.

Morgan, John T. 1986. "The Decline of Log House Construction in Blount County, Tennessee." PhD dissertation. Department of Geography, University of Tennessee.

———. 1990. *The Log House in East Tennessee*. Knoxville: University of Tennessee Press.

———. 1997. "The Cantilever Barn in Southwest Virginia." In *Diversity and Accommodation: Essays on the Cultural Composition of the Virginia Frontier*, ed. Michael J. Puglisi, 275–94. Knoxville: University of Tennessee Press.

Morgan, John, and Ashby Lynch Jr. 1984. "The Log Barns of Blount County, Tennessee." *Tennessee Anthropologist* 9 (2): 85–103.

Morgan, John, and Joy Medford. 1980. "Log Houses in Grainger County, Tennessee." *Tennessee Anthropologist* 5 (2):137–58.

Morrison, Hugh. 1952. *Early American Architecture*. New York: Dover.

Naismith, Robert J. 1985. *Buildings of the Scottish Countryside*. London: Victor Gollancz.

National Geographic Society. 1988. *Historical Atlas of the United States*. Washington, DC: National Geographic Society.

Newton, Milton. 1974. "Cultural Preadaptation and the Upland South." In *Man and Cultural Heritage: Papers in Honor of Fred B. Kniffen*, vol. 5, *Geoscience and Man*, ed. H. J. Walker and W. G. Haag, 143–54. Baton Rouge: School of Geoscience, Louisiana State University.

———. 1989. "Dogtrot House." In *Encyclopedia of Southern Culture*, ed. Charles Reagan Wilson and William Ferris Jr. Chapel Hill: University of North Carolina Press.

Newton, Milton B., Jr., and Linda Pulliam-DiNapoli. 1977. "Log Houses as Public Occasions: A Historical Theory." *Annals of the Association of American Geographers* 67: 360–83.

Noble, Allen G. 1984. *Wood, Brick, and Stone: The North American Settlement Landscape.* 2 vols. Amherst: University of Massachusetts Press.

———. 1992. *To Build in a New Land: Ethnic Landscapes in North America.* Baltimore: Johns Hopkins University Press.

Noble, Allen G., and Richard K. Cleek. 1995. *The Old Barn Book: A Field Guide to North American Barns and Other Farm Structures.* New Brunswick, NJ: Rutgers University Press.

Olson, Ted. 1998. *Blue Ridge Folklore.* Jackson: University Press of Mississippi.

O'Malley, James Ross. 1972. "The 'I' House: An Indicator of Agricultural Opulence in Upper East Tennessee." Master's thesis. Department of Geography, University of Tennessee.

———. 1977. "The 'I' House: An Indicator of Agricultural Attainment in the Southern Appalachian Valley." In *West Virginia and Appalachia: Selected Readings,* ed. Howard G. Adkins. Dubuque, IA: Kendall-Hunt.

O'Malley, James R., and John B. Rehder. 1978. "The Two-Story Log House in the Upland South." *Journal of Popular Culture* 11: 904–15.

Patton, Charles V. 1948. "Old Timers Tell of Strange Tale of Yellow Springs 'Lost' Hotel." *Knoxville Journal,* April 27, 1948.

Pillsbury, Richard. 1976. "The Construction Materials of the Rural Folk Housing of the Pennsylvania Culture Region." *Pioneer America* 8 (2): 98–106.

Pillsbury, Richard, and Andrew Kardos. 1970. *A Field Guide to the Folk Architecture in the Northeast.* Hanover, NH: Dartmouth College.

Ramsey, J. G. M. [1853] 1926. *The Annals of Tennessee.* Kingsport, TN: Kingsport Press.

Reding, William M. 2002. "Assessment of Spatial and Temporal Patterns in Log Structures in East Tennessee." Master's thesis. Department of Geography, University of Tennessee.

Rehder, John B. 1992. "The Scotch Irish and English in Appalachia." In *To Build in a New Land: Ethnic Landscapes in North America,* ed. Allen G. Noble, 95–118. Baltimore: Johns Hopkins University Press.

———. 1997a. "Scotch-Irish." In *American Immigrant Cultures,* ed. David Levinson and Melvin Ember, 767–73. New York: Simon and Schuster Macmillan.

———. 1997b. "Scots." In *American Immigrant Cultures,* ed. David Levinson and Melvin Ember, 773–79. New York: Simon and Schuster Macmillan.

———. 1999. *Delta Sugar: Louisiana's Vanishing Plantation Landscape.* Baltimore: Johns Hopkins University Press.

———. 2004. *Appalachian Folkways.* Baltimore: Johns Hopkins University Press.

———. 2005. "Hensley, Kentucky: A Twentieth-Century Pioneer Folk Settlement." *Material Culture* 37 (1): 107–30.

———. 2006. *Union County, Tennessee Narrative for 'Between Fences.'* Nashville: Humanities Tennessee.

Rehder, John B., John Morgan, and Joy L. Medford. 1979. "The Decline of Smokehouses in Grainger County, Tennessee." *West Georgia College Studies in the Social Sciences* 18: 75–83.

Rehder, Karen. 1989. "Observations of Folk Houses as Found in the Eastern Tennessee Region." Unpublished data in Special Collections, John C. Hodges Library, University of Tennessee.

Riedl, Norbert F., Donald B. Ball, and Anthony P. Cavender. 1976. *A Survey of Traditional Architecture and Related Material Folk Culture Patterns in the Normandy Reservoir, Coffee County, Tennessee*. Department of Anthropology Report of Investigations, no. 17. Knoxville: University of Tennessee and Tennessee Valley Authority.

Roberts, Warren. 1985. *Log Buildings of Southern Indiana*. Bloomington, IN: Trickster Press.

Rogers, Steve. 2008. Digital image communications, Feb. 7.

Rouse, Parke, Jr. 1995. *The Great Wagon Road*. Richmond, VA: Dietz Press.

Save Castalian Springs! blog. 2011. http://savecastaliansprings.blogspot.com/.

Schimmer, James R., and Allen G. Noble. 1984. "The Evolution of the Corn Crib." *Pioneer America Society Transactions* 7: 21–33.

Scofield, Edna. 1936. "The Evolution and Development of Tennessee Houses." *Journal of the Tennessee Academy of Science* 11 (4): 229–40.

Sevier County, Tennessee. *Warranty Deed Book* 2319, p. 161.

Shurtleff, Harold R. 1939. *The Log Cabin Myth: A Study of the Dwellings of the English Colonists in North America*. Cambridge, MA: Harvard University Press.

Stupka, Arthur. 1964. *Trees, Shrubs, and Woody Vines of the Great Smoky Mountains National Park*. Knoxville: University of Tennessee Press.

Tennessee Historical Commission. 1996. *Tennessee Historical Markers*. Nashville: Tennessee Historical Commission.

Tolley, Lynn. "Jack Daniel Distillery." In *The Tennessee Encyclopedia of History and Culture*, ed. Carroll Van West, 467. Nashville: Tennessee Historical Society and Rutledge Hill Press.

Upton, Dell, ed. 1986. *America's Architectural Roots: Ethnic Groups That Built America*. Washington, DC: Preservation Press.

Upton, Dell. 1989. "Vernacular Architecture—Upland South." In *Encyclopedia of Southern Culture*, ed. Charles Reagan Wilson and William R. Ferris Jr., 113–15. Chapel Hill: University of North Carolina Press.

Upton, Dell, and John Michael Vlach, eds. 1986. *Common Places: Readings in American Vernacular Architecture*. Athens: University of Georgia Press.

Venable, Sam. 2000. *Mountain Hands: A Portrait of Southern Appalachia*. Knoxville: University of Tennessee Press.

Vlach, John Michael. 1986. "The Shotgun House: An African Architectural Legacy." In *Common Places: Readings in American Vernacular Architecture*, ed. Del Upton and John Michael Vlach, 58–78. Athens: University of Georgia Press.

———. 1993. *Back of the Big House: The Architecture of Plantation Slavery*. Chapel Hill: University of North Carolina Press.

Wertenbaker, Thomas J. 1938. *The Founding of American Civilization: The Middle Colonies*. New York: Charles Scribner's Sons.

Weslager, C. A. 1969. *The Log Cabin in America*. New Brunswick, NJ: Rutgers University Press.

West, Carroll Van, ed. 1998. *Tennessee History: The Land, the People, and the Culture*. Knoxville: University of Tennessee Press.

West, Carroll Van. 1995. *Tennessee's Historic Landscapes: A Traveler's Guide*. Knoxville: University of Tennessee Press.

Wilhelm, Eugene J., Jr. 1978."Folk Settlements in the Blue Ridge Mountains." *Appalachian Journal* 5 (2): 204–45.

Williams, Michael Ann. 1995. *Great Smoky Mountains Folklife.* Jackson: University Press of Mississippi.

Williams, Samuel Cole. 1937. *Dawn of Tennessee Valley and Tennessee History.* Johnson City, TN: Watauga Press.

Wilson, Charles Reagan, and William R. Ferris Jr., eds. 1989. *Encyclopedia of Southern Culture.* Chapel Hill: University of North Carolina Press.

Wilson, Eugene M. 1970. "The Single Pen House in the South." *Pioneer America* 2 (1): 21–28.

———. 1971. "Some Similarities Between American and European Folk Houses." *Pioneer America* 3 (2): 8–14.

———. 1975. *Alabama Folk Houses.* Montgomery: Alabama Historical Commission.

Work Projects Administration. [1939] 1986. *The WPA Guide to Tennessee.* Knoxville: University of Tennessee Press.

Wright, Martin. 1958. "The Antecedents of the Double-Pen House Type." *Annals of the Association of American Geographers* 48: 109–17.

Zelinsky, Wilbur. 1992. *The Cultural Geography of the United States.* Rev. ed. Englewood Cliffs, NJ: Prentice Hall.

Index

Page numbers in **boldface** refer to photographs and other illustrations. All counties are located in Tennessee.

Alfred's cabin (Hermitage), 18, 132
American Backwoods Frontier, The (Jordan and Kaups), 42, 68, 71–72
Appalachia. *See* Southern Appalachia
apple houses, 103–4
architecture. *See* folk architecture
arc sawing, as age indicator, 14
ash logs, as building material, for Wynnewood, 122

Ball, Donald, 62
balloon framing construction, 64, 78, 79
barns, log, 39, 83–97; typology of, 5, 83–84, **85**. *See also* corncribs, log; *and specific types of log barns and individual farms by names*
Bean, William, 32
Belle Meade Plantation (Davidson County), 132
Birdwell, Michael E., *Upper Cumberland Historic Architecture*, 70
blacksmith shops, **105,** 106
Bledsoe, Isaac, 121
Bledsoe's Lick, 117–18, 123
Bledsoe's Lick Historical Park, 77, 131–32

blockhouses, log, 16–17, **30,** 131
Blount, William, 18; mansion of, 42
Blue Ridge Province (Tennessee), 27, 31
board-and-batten construction, 79–80; Meek Williams place, 126, 127; Wynnewood, 121
Boone, Daniel, 31
box framing construction, 41
box houses, 39, 78–82, **81**
bricks, as building materials: for four-pen houses, 78; for I-houses, 73, 75
Brown, Jacob, 32
bungalows, 39, 78–82, **80**
Byrd, William, *History of the Dividing Line*, 42

Cades Cove (Great Smoky Mountains National Park), 131
Cage, William, 123
canning houses, 103–4
cantilever log barns, 91–97, **92, 94,** 100, **132;** diagram, **85;** foundations, 89, 93, **93,** 94; regional patterns, 94–97
capital, Tennessee territorial (Rocky Mount), 18, 131
Carmichael Inn (Loudon County), **76**
Carter, John, 32
Carter's Valley settlement (Tennessee), 32, 36

Castalian Springs, 117–18, 123
Castalian Springs Hotel (Sumner County), 121–22. *See also* Wynnewood (Sumner County)
Cavender, Tony, 62
Cedar Bluff Stables (Knox County), 112–13. *See also* Walker Springs place (Knox County)
cedar logs, as building material, 55, 122, 127
cellar buildings, **103,** 103–4
cemeteries, determining buildings' ages from, 14
Cherokee Indians: European conflicts with, 29; log construction by, 41, 55; removal from Tennessee, 37, 69
Chesapeake area (Maryland and Virginia), log buildings in, 41–42
chestnut logs, as building material, 55, 127; as age indicator, 60; for barns, 90; for houses, 60, 65
chicken coops, 104
chimney(s): as age indicator, 14; brick, 14; on bungalows and box houses, 78, 79; cinderblock, 14; on double-pen log houses, 62, **63,** 64, **65,** 67; on Hamilton-Tolliver place, 116, **118**; on I-houses, 74–75, 76; on Meek Williams place, 124; mud-and-stick, 22, **23**; sandstone, 21; on single-pen log houses, 56, 60, 62; stone, 14, 33; on Walker Springs place, 115; on Wynnewood, 119, 121
churches, 106–8, **107, 109**
circular sawing, as age indicator, 14
clapboard siding, 41
Congressional Reservation (Tennessee), European settlement in, 37
corncribs, log, 84, **85, 86,** 92, 104, **126**
corner notches. *See* notches
Cragfont mansion (Sumner County), 77, **77,** 123, 132
crib (barn) units, log, 39, 83, 89, 91–92, 96
crosscut sawing, as age indicator, 14
Cumberland double-pen log houses, 39, 40, 62–64, **63,** 111; diagram, **57**; regional patterns, 56, 63–64; Walker Springs place, 111–15, **112, 113,** 131
Cumberland Gap, settlement of, 31
Cumberland Plateau (Tennessee), 27

Cumberland Settlements (Tennessee), 25, 34–36, 37

Daniel, Jasper "Jack," distillery (Moore County), 102
Deep South. *See* Lowland South
dendrochronology, **15,** 15–18, 113–14, 115, 129
Depression houses, 4, 43, 80–81, 109
diamond notches, 41, 49–51, **51**; regional patterns, 50–51, 54, 55
Dickinson, W. Calvin, *Upper Cumberland Historic Architecture,* 70
Doe Creek School (Henderson County), 110
dogtrot double-pen log houses, 39, 40, 62, 66–72; Belle Meade Plantation, 132; diagram, **57**; double-crib barns resembling, 86; examples, **10, 67, 68**; John White's house, **70,** 70–71; origins, 67, 71–72; regional patterns, 56, 67–68, 71; Wynnewood's elements, 118
dogtrot passages, 70, **74,** 113, 119, 120–21
Donelson, John, settlement group led by, 35–36; map of route, **36**
doors: deep-threshold, 125; gable-end, 67, 97, 104, 106; log cabin, 40; single-pen house, 56
double-crib log barns, 23, 86–89, **88**; cantilevered, 93–94; correlated with double-pen log houses, 86; diagram, **85**; on Meek Williams place, 126, **126, 128,** 129; regional patterns, 87, 89
double notches, 3, 53, 55
double-pen log houses, 39, 62–72, 81, 124; correlated with double-crib barns, 86; diagram, **57**; regional patterns, 56; with uneven pens, 71. *See also* Cumberland double-pen log houses; dogtrot double-pen log houses; saddlebag double-pen log houses
Durham, Walter, *Wynnewood: Bledsoe's Castalian Springs, Tennessee,* 117–18
Dyer, Crockett and Cautella, 112

Eastern Highland Rim (Tennessee), 27
eastern red cedar logs, as building material, determining age from, 18

East Tennessee, 27, 28; European settlement patterns, 25, 29, 31–33, 37
English settlers, 25, 26; construction methods, 41–42, 58, 74–75; notch styles used by, 49; regional settlement patterns, 25, 26, 29, 30, 31
English Tidewater region, 26, 27, 31
European settlers: barn types linked to, 91, 95, 96, 100; construction methods, 46, 55; regional settlement patterns, 28, 29, 30–33, 43. *See also* English settlers; Finnish settlers; German settlers; Scandinavian settlers; Scotch-Irish settlers; Swedish settlers

farmsteads, 29. *See also individual farms by names*
Faulkner, Charles, 113
fieldwork: experiences during, 5–8, 18–24, 116; procedures, 9–10, 12–15
Finnish settlers: construction methods, 42, 55; notch styles used by, 49
floors: dirt, 1, 4, 39, 40, 83, 92, 106; stone, 102; threshing, 92; wooden, 83, 104
folk architecture, 1–24; acculturation in, 49; construction techniques and materials, 1, 40, 56, 83; fieldwork on, 5–8, 18–24, 116; in Southern Appalachia, 4, 39–40, 42–43, 127; timber types, 54–55; traditions in, 3–5. *See also* barns, log; log buildings; log houses; notches; outbuildings, log; Tennessee Historical Commission (THC), historic buildings survey
Fort Marr (Polk County), 16, **30**, 131
Fort Nashborough (Tennessee), 34
four-crib log barns, 89–90, **90**; diagram, **85**; regional patterns, 91
four-pen log houses, 39, 78, **79**, 124; diagram, **57**
Fox, Todd, 99
framed-timber construction outbuildings, 101–2, 103, 104
French Lick settlement (Tennessee), 34
French Louisiana, 26, 27
full-dovetail notches, 41, 49, **50**; as age indicator, 14; regional patterns, 54, 55

gables: on barns, 86, 93; on houses, **65,** 78, 79, **119**; on outbuildings, 97, 98, 101, 103. *See also* roofs
Gavin, Michael, 51
gear sheds, 84, **87**; diagram, **85**
German settlers: barn types linked to, 95, 96, 100; construction methods, 76, 86, 97; notch styles used by, 42, 43, 46, 48–49, 55; patterns of settlement, 25, 29, 30, 32–33, 99
Gevel, Saskia L. van de, 113–14
Gillespie stone house (Greene County), 76
Glassie, Henry: cabin research, 42, 58; on dogtrot houses, 71; on four-crib barns, 89, 91; on outbuildings, 97
Governor John Sevier Plantation (Knox County). *See* Marble Springs Plantation (Knox County)
Graham, William, 76–77
Graham house (Claiborne County), 76–77
granaries, 83, 104, **105**
Great Depression, log house construction during, 4, 43, 80–81, 109
Great Smoky Mountain Heritage Museum (Blount County), 131, **133**
Great Smoky Mountains National Park, 59–60, 131; Ogle farm in, 64–65, **65, 66,** 89–90, **90**
Great Valley (Tennessee), European settlement in, 28, 30, 31–32, 43
Great Wagon Road, 30, 32
Greenbrier School (Blount County), 108, 131
Grissino-Mayer, Henri D., 113–14
gristmills, 65, 106

half-dovetail notches, 41, 46–49, **48,** 52; as age indicator, 14, 15, 16, 60; on barns, 94; on blockhouses, **30**; on churches, **107,** 108, **109**; on Hamilton-Tolliver place, 116; on houses, 58, 59, 60, **61,** 62, 70; on outbuildings, 99, **100,** 106; regional patterns, 48–49, 54, 55; on schoolhouses, 109, 110; on smokehouses, 98; on Whaley Place, 12
hall-and-parlor houses, 42, 71
Hamilton-Tolliver Place (Union County), 116, **117, 118**

hearths. *See* Cumberland Settlements (Tennessee); settlement history; Watauga Settlements (Tennessee)
Heinrich Ernst (Henry Earnest) log house (Greene County), 33, **34**
Hermitage (Nashville), 18, 132
History of the Dividing Line (Byrd), 42
hog enclosures, log, 17; Meek Williams place, 126, 127
The Homeplace-1850 (Stewart County), 132
Hope, Thomas, 76
houses. *See* log houses
house-that-moved. *See* Walker Springs place (Knox County)
Hulan, Richard, on dogtrot houses, 71
Hurst, Elvin, 130

I-houses, 39, 40, 72–77, **73, 74, 75**; building materials, 72, 73, 75–77, 78; Carmichael Inn, **76**; Cragfont mansion, 77, **77**, 123, 132; determining ages of, 16; evolution, **57**; log, 118, 124; origins, 74–75; regional patterns, 71–72, 75, 77; stone, 73, 75–77, **77**, 82; Walker Springs place, 78

Jack Daniel's Distillery (Moore County), 102
Jesse Gambill farm, 99
John White House (White County), **70**, 70–71
Jones, Robbie, 100
Jordan, Terry G., 74, 86; *The American Backwoods Frontier*, 42, 68, 71–72

Kaups, Matti, *The American Backwoods Frontier*, 42, 68, 71–72
Kemp, Homer D., *Upper Cumberland Historic Architecture*, 70
Kentucky Bluegrass Basin, 27
Kephart, Horace, 40
Kivett, John, 77
Kniffen, Fred B., 42; on dogtrot houses, 67, 71; on I-houses, 72–73

land use, European *vs.* Native American views of, 29

Layman (Lehmann) farm (Sevier County), 99, 100
Lincoln Logs (toys), 3, 53
lofts: in barns, **85, 92,** 93, 96; in houses, 56
log buildings, 2–3; blockhouses, 16–17, **30,** 131; churches, 106–8, **107, 109**; commercial, 4–5, 21; determining ages of, 13–18, 60, 129–30; exceptional examples, 111–30; loss of, 132, 134; modern, 4–5; origins, 40–43; preservation of, **75, 133**; schools, 108–10; traditional construction methods, 3–5; two-level cantilevered, 99-100; types of, 11; visiting, 131–34. *See also* barns, log; outbuildings, log; sawn-lumber construction; timber-frame construction
log houses, 4, 39–82, 83; cabins, **2,** 3, **3,** 18, 39–40, 58; construction methods, 41, 64, 75, 78, 79, 101–2; determining ages of, 14, **16,** 18; exceptional examples, 111–30; log cabins, 39–40; notch styles used on, 43–54, 55; origins, 40–43; timber types, 11, 54–55; twentieth-century, 78–82; typology, 5, 56–78, **57**; visiting, 131–32; Watauga Settlement, 33. *See also* chimney(s); doors; floors; gables, on houses; *and specific types of log houses and individual houses by names*
logs: hewn, 4, **47,** 73; split, 41, 53; squared, 41, 45, 46, **47,** 92. *See also* notches; timber; *and specific types of logs*
logs, round: on barns, 92; determining ages of, 14; on I-houses, 73; notch styles used on, 41, 43, **44,** 45, **45,** 53, 54; on schoolhouses, 109, **110**
Lowland South, 25, 26, 27–28; map, **26**

Mann, David F., 99
Mansker's Station (Davidson County), 132
Marble Springs Plantation (Knox County), 18, 113–15, **114,** 131
Mauris-Earnest Fort House (Greene County), 33, **34**
McMahon, Thomas DeArnold Wilson, cantilever barn built by, 92
Meek Williams place (Sevier County), **8,** 124–30, **125, 126, 128**

Middle Tennessee, 27; patterns of settlement in, 34–36, 37
Moffett, Marian. *See* Moffett-Wodehouse barn survey
Moffett-Wodehouse barn survey, 93–94, 95, 96
Morgan, John T.: barn surveys, 89, 95n, 96, 100; house surveys, 68–69, 79
mortise-and-tenon joinery, 41, 56, **59**, 70, 115, 120
Museum of Appalachia (Anderson County), 131, **132**

Nakanawa summer camp (Cumberland County), 20–21, **21**
Nashville, Tennessee, origins, 34, 36, 37
Nashville Basin (Tennessee), 27; settlement patterns in, 28, 34–36
Native Americans, European conflicts with, 29. *See also* Cherokee Indians Netherland Inn (Sullivan County), 131
Nolichucky Settlement (Tennessee), 32, 36
North Carolina, Tennessee's independence from, 33
North Carolina Military Reservation, 37
North Carolina Peidmont, settlement of, 31
North Holston settlement (Tennessee), 32, 36
notches: as age indicator, 14; origins, 42–43, 55; regional patterns, 53–54; typology, 5, 11, 41, 43–54, **52**. *See also specific types of notches and under specific types of buildings and species of wood*

oak logs, as building material: for barns, 24; for churches, **107**, 108; determining age based on, 18, 60; Hamilton-Tolliver place, 116; Heinrich Ernst house, **34**; houses, 33, 58, 59, 60, 62; Meek Williams place, 127; notch styles used on, 46, 47; regional patterns, 55; schoolhouses, 109; Walker Springs place, 115; Wynnewood, 122, **123**
Ogle, Noah "Bud," 64–65
Ogle farm (Great Smoky Mountains National Park), 64–65, **65, 66**, 131; barn, 89–90, **90**

Okolona Church (Overton County), **107**, 108
Old Dutch Settlement (Sevier County), 99
Old Union Church (Overton County), 108
Old Union Meeting House (Overton County), 108, **109**
Old Union United Methodist Church (Hawkins County), **107**, 108
O'Malley, Jim, 116; "The Two-Story Log House in the Upland South," 73–74
outbuildings, log, 5, 83–110; barns, 5, 39, 83–97; blacksmith shops, **105**, 106; cantilever-style, 95, 97; cellar buildings, **103**, 103–4; chicken coops, 104; corncribs, 84, **85, 86**, 92, 104, **126**; framed timber, 101–2, 103, 104; granaries, 83, 104, **105**; gristmills, 65, 106; Meek Williams place, 126–29; notch styles used on, 45, 46, 47; single-crib, 97; springhouses, 65, 101–2; two-level cantilevered, 99–100. *See also* smokehouses, log; springhouses, log

Pennsylvania region: barn types linked to, 95, 100; construction methods linked to, 55, 86; folk architecture in, 42–43; outbuilding types linked to, 97; settlers from, 30, 31–32, 32–33, 49
pen (house) units, 39, 56, 83. *See also* log houses
Perron, Ann, 20, 21
pine logs, as building material: as age indicator, 60; for barns, 23; for blockhouses, **30**; determining age based on, 14, 60; for houses, 55, 58, 59–60, 81, **81**; for Meek Williams place, 127; notch styles used on, 33, 43, **44**, 46, 53–54, 55; for outbuildings, 99, **100**; for schoolhouses, 109, **110**
pole barns, 4, 89
poplar logs, as building material: determining age from, 60; for houses, 55, 60; notch styles used on, 45, 54. *See also* yellow poplar logs, as building material
potato houses, 103

Ramsey, Francis A., 76
Ramsey, J. G. M., 40

Ramsey house (Knox County), 76
red oak logs, as building material, determining age from, 18. See also oak logs, as building material
Rehder, John B., "The Two-Story Log House in the Upland South," 73–74
Rice, L. L., 21
Ridge and Valley Province (Tennessee), 27, 31; patterns of settlement, 28, 30, 43
Riedl, Norbert F., 62
Roaring Fork Motor Nature Trail (Great Smoky Mountains National Park), 131
Roberts, Stephen R., 123
Robertson, James, settlement party led by, 31, 32, 35–36; map of route, **36**
Rocky Mount (Sullivan County), Tennessee territorial capital at, 18, 131
rod (British unit of measurement), 58
Rogan house (Bledsoe Lick Historical Park), 77
roofs: Alpine, 86, **86, 88,** 97, 101; cantilevered, 99; gable, 78, 89, 98; on Hamilton-Tolliver place, 116; projected diagnostic, 98, 103; saddle, 62, 78, 86, **88,** 93; single-slanted, 104; on Wynnewood, 120. See also gables; gear sheds
root cellars, 103–4

saddlebag double-pen log houses, 39, 40, 62, 64–66; determining ages of, 14; diagram, **57**; framed, 82; Hamilton-Tolliver place, 116, **117**; Meek Williams place, 124–30, **125, 126**; Ogle farm, 64–65, **65, 66,** 131; regional patterns, 56, 65–66; twentieth-century, 81; Wynnewood's elements of, 118, 119, 120
saddle notches, 43–45; as age indicator, 14; on houses, 4, 58, 81, **81**; on Meek Williams place, 127; on outbuildings, 46; regional patterns, 44–45, 53, 54, 55; on round logs, 41, **44**; on schoolhouses, 109, **110**
saddle-V notches, 45–46; as age indicator, 14; on barns, 23, 24, **91**; on houses, 4, 59; on Meek Williams place, 127; regional patterns, 46, 54, 55; on round logs, 41, **45**
Sam Houston Schoolhouse (Blount County), 108
saw marks, as age indicators, 14

sawmills, 14, 40, 96, **132**
sawn-lumber construction: for houses, 64, 73, 75, 78, 81; for lofts, 96; on Meek Williams place, 126, 127; for outbuildings, 101, 103, 104; regional patterns, 41; for weatherboarding, 91, 93, 111
Scandinavian settlers: construction methods, 42, 71–72; notch styles used by, 46, 49, 53, 55
schools, log, 108–10, **110**; regional patterns, 108
Schraeder farm (Sevier County), 100
Scotch-Irish settlers: construction methods, 41, 58, 97; notch styles used by, 42–43, 49; patterns of settlement, 25, 26, 29, 30, 32–33
semilunate-crown notches, 41, 53; regional patterns, 55
settlement history, 25–37, 43, 99. See also *individual ethnic groups*
Sevier, John, 31, 32, 113. See also Marble Springs Plantation (Knox County)
Shelby, Evan, 32
shotgun houses, 78
single-crib log barns, 84, **86,** 89; diagram, **85**; with gear sheds, 84, **87**
single-pen log houses, **2, 13,** 56–62, **59,** 124; determining ages of, 18, 60, 62; diagram, **57**; notch styles used on, 58–60, **61**; regional patterns, 12, 39, 40, 56, 58; Sevier's house, 18, 113–14; Whaley Place, 12; Wynnewood's elements of, 121, 124
slave cabins, 18, 32
slaves, 26, 27, 35, 74, 122, 124
slight framing construction, 41
Smith, Seth, 76
smokehouses, log, 84, 97–99, **98,** 103; determining ages of, 16; on Meek Williams place, 126, 127, 129; regional patterns, 99; two-level, **100, 101**; on Wynnewood property, 121, 122
South, the, cultural context, 25–31
southeastern Tennessee, European settlement, 37
Southern Appalachia, 25–26; cultural characteristics of, 7, 127; folk architecture, 4, 39-40, 42–43, 127; notch styles used in, 46, 48–49; patterns of settlement, 30–31, 43, 96; Tennessee's portion of, 27
Southern Florida, 27

springhouses, log, 65, 101–2, **102**, 103; cantilevered, 17, **17**, 99; regional patterns, 102
square notches, 41, 51–52; on barns, 94; on houses, 59; regional patterns, 52, 55; on smokehouses, 98
Stanley Valley (Hawkins County), **7**
State of Franklin (Tennessee), 33
stations (farmsteads), 29. *See also individual farms by names*
stone, as building material: for cellars, 103, 104; for four-pen houses, 78; for I-houses, 73, 75–77, **77**, 82; for springhouses, 101–2
Stone Mountain School (Hawkins County), 109–10, **110**
stovepipes, 14, 78
Swaggerty Blockhouse (Cocke County), 16–17, **17**, 99
Swedish settlers: construction methods, 42; notch styles used by, 49, 55
Sycamore Shoals settlement (Tennessee), 32

Tennessee: forest ecology, 54–55; maps, xiv, **28**; settlement history, 25–37, 43, 99
Tennessee Historical Commission (THC), historic buildings survey, 5, 9–18, 24; barns, 94, 95; houses, 116; notch types, 43; timber types, 54
Tennessee's Historic Landscapes: A Traveler's Guide (West), 33
Tidewater region. *See* English Tidewater region
timber: as age indicator, 14; typology of, 11, 54–55
timber-frame construction, 41, 75, 101–2
tools, hand, 1, 40, 83
Trail of Tears (1837-38), 37, 69
transverse-crib barns, 89, 90–91, **91**; diagram, **85**; notch styles used for, 24; regional patterns, 91
trees, determining ages of, **15**, 15–18, 113–14, 115, 129
twelve-sided log building (Nakanawa summer camp), 20–21, **21**
two-level cantilevered log outbuildings, 99–100; regional patterns, 100
two-pen log houses. *See* double-pen log houses

"Two-Story Log House in the Upland South, The" (O'Malley and Rehder), 73–74

Underwood, Chris, **8,** 129
Upland South, 25–26, 27; map, **26**
Upper Cumberland Historic Architecture (Dickinson, Birdwell, Kemp), 70
Upper East Tennessee, European settlement in, 25, 29, 31–33, 37. *See also* Rocky Mount, Tennessee territorial capital at

vernacular architecture, 1–2, 67, 72. *See also* folk architecture
Vernacular Architecture Forum (VAF), 1–2
V notches: as age indicator, 14, 16; on barns, 94; on churches, 108; Heinrich Ernst house, **34**; on hewn logs, 41, 46, **47**; on houses, **16**, 33, 58, 59, 60, 71; regional patterns, 54, 55; on smokehouses, 16, 98; Wynnewood, 122, **123**

Walker Sisters place (Great Smoky Mountains National Park), 131
Walker Springs place (Knox County), 111–15, **112, 113**, 131
walnut logs, as building material, for Wynnewood, 122, **123**
Watauga Settlements (Tennessee), 25, 31–33, 36, 37, 104
weatherboarding: on barns, 91, **92,** 94; on houses, 19, 62, **112**; on Meek Williams place, 125, 126; notches obscured by, 43; sawn-lumber, 91, 93, 111
West, Carroll Van, 76; *Tennessee's Historic Landscapes: A Traveler's Guide*, 33
Western Highland Rim (Tennessee), 27
West Tennessee, 27–28, 37
Whaley Place (Jefferson County), 12
White, John, 70–71
Wigwam, The (Nakanawa summer camp), 20–21, **21**
Wilderness Road, 31, 32
Williams, Elsie, 125, 129, 130
Williams, Meek, 125, 129–30
Williams, Michael Ann, 79
Williams, Samuel Cole, 32
Wilson, Eugene M., on dogtrot houses, 71

Winchester, James, 77; estate of, 121, 123. *See also* Wynnewood (Sumner County)
Winchester, Valerius Publicola, 123
Wodehouse, Lawrence. *See* Moffett-Wodehouse barn survey
wood. *See* logs; timber; trees, determining ages of; *and individual species of logs*
Wright, Martin, on dogtrot houses, 71
Wynne, Alfred Royal, 122, 123, 124
Wynne, Almira Winchester, 122, 123
Wynne, George Winchester, 124
Wynnewood (Sumner County), 74, 116–24, **119, 122, 123,** 131; diagram, **120**
Wynnewood: Bledsoe's Castalian Springs, Tennessee (Durham), 117–18

yellow poplar logs, as building material, 54–55, 127; as age indicator, 14, 15, 60; for churches, **109**; for houses, **16,** 58, 59, 60, **61,** 62, 70, 71; notch styles used on, 12, 43, 46, 47; for outbuildings, 106; for schoolhouses, 109, 110

Tennessee Log Buildings was designed and typeset on a Macintosh OSX computer system using InDesign CS5 software. The body text is set in 9.75/14 ITC Century Std and display type is set in Bauhaus Std Demi. This book was designed and typeset by Barbara Karwhite and manufactured by Thomson-Shore, Inc.